Better Homes and Gardens®

CHRISTMAS
COOKING
FROM THE HEART™

Traditions with a Twist

Meredith® Books
Des Moines, Iowa

Better Homes and Gardens®
CHRISTMAS COOKING
FROM THE HEART™

Editor: Jessica Saari
Contributing Editor: Linda J. Henry
Contributing Writer: Cynthia Pearson
Contributing Designer: Angie Haupert Hoogensen
Copy Chief: Doug Kouma
Copy Editor: Kevin Cox
Publishing Operations Manager: Karen Schirm
Edit and Design Production Coordinator: Mary Lee Gavin
Editorial Assistant: Sheri Cord
Book Production Managers: Marjorie J. Schenkelberg, Mark Weaver
Contributing Copy Editor: Carol DeMasters
Contributing Proofreaders: Jean Baker, Judy Friedman, Karen Grossman
Contributing Photographers: Marty Baldwin, Scott Little, Blaine Moats
Contributing Prop Stylist: Sue Mitchell
Contributing Recipe Development: Ellen Boeke, Linda J. Henry, Tami Leonard, Shelli McConnell
Contributing Food Stylists: Greg Luna, Angela McCrovitz, Dianna Nolin
Test Kitchen Director: Lynn Blanchard
Test Kitchen Product Supervisor: Jill Moberly
Test Kitchen Culinary Specialists: Marilyn Cornelius, Juliana Hale, Maryellyn Krantz,
Colleen Weeden, Lori Wilson
Test Kitchen Nutrition Specialists: Elizabeth Burt, R.D., L.D.; Laura Marzen, R.D., L.D.

Meredith® Books
Editorial Director: John Riha
Deputy Editor: Jennifer Darling
Managing Editor: Kathleen Armentrout
Brand Manager: Janell Pittman
Group Editor: Jan Miller
Senior Associate Design Director: Mick Schnepf

Director, Marketing and Publicity: Amy Nichols
Executive Director, Sales: Ken Zagor
Director, Operations: George A. Susral
Director, Production: Douglas M. Johnston
Business Director: Janice Croat

Vice President and General Manager, SIM: Jeff Myers

Better Homes and Gardens® Magazine
Editor in Chief: Gayle Goodson Butler
Senior Deputy Editor, Home Design: Oma Blaise Ford
Deputy Editor, Food and Entertaining: Nancy Wall Hopkins

Meredith Publishing Group
President: Jack Griffin
President, Better Homes and Gardens®: Andy Sareyan
Vice President, Corporate Solutions: Michael Brownstein
Vice President, Manufacturing: Bruce Heston
Vice President, Consumer Marketing: David Ball
Director, Creative Services: Grover Kirkman
Consumer Product Marketing Director: Steve Swanson
Consumer Product Marketing Manager: Wendy Merical
Business Director: Jim Leonard

Meredith Corporation
Chairman of the Board: William T. Kerr
President and Chief Executive Officer: Stephen M. Lacy

In Memoriam: E.T. Meredith III (1933–2003)

Test Kitchen

Our seal assures you that every recipe in *Christmas Cooking from the Heart*™ has been tested in the Better Homes and Gardens® Test Kitchen. This means that each recipe is practical and reliable, and meets our high standards of taste appeal. We guarantee your satisfaction with this book for as long as you own it.

All of us at Meredith® Books are dedicated to providing you with information and ideas to enhance your home. We welcome your comments and suggestions. Write to us at: Meredith Books Editorial Department, 1716 Locust St., Des Moines, IA 50309-3023. *Christmas Cooking from the Heart* is available by mail. To order editions from past years, call 800/627-5490.

Cover Photography:
Front cover: White Chocolate-Peppermint Dream Cake (page 88)
Back cover: Candy Cane Sugar Cookies (page 150)
Produced by: Catherine Brett and Lois White
Photographer: Pete Krumhardt
Food Stylist: Jennifer Peterson

Candy canes courtesy of Hammond's Candies
www.hammondscandies.com

table of contents

Chocolatey Butter-Nut
Cinnamon Rolls, page 66

Apricot-Apple Stuffed
Crown Roast, page 8

special traditions

Despite the heartfelt satisfaction, not to mention anticipation, that comes with savoring special dishes that are enjoyed but once or twice a year, sometimes we want to put a new flavor twist on our traditional menus. The creative cook who wants to offer something a little different will find a multitude of recipes here.

Christmas Cooking from the Heart: Traditions with a Twist answers the call so splendidly. Just imagine a kitchen counter stocked with a spread of ingredients and cupboards fully equipped with the pans and tools to produce familiar forms. But then a little elf begins to dance amid the mix, splashing some eggnog into the French toast dip, tossing Italian seasonings onto the turkey, plopping jalapeño jelly into the butter cookie batter, and whoops, now apple butter slips into the pumpkin pie. Then everything slides into the hot oven, and mouth-watering aromas fill the house.

If you want to do things a little differently, this book is your resource. You will find jazzed-up, refreshed recipes for everything from breakfast and brunch to afternoon tea and New Year's parties, and lots and lots of cookies and sweets. This year, do everything a little differently, or work in a fresh recipe or two with your favorites. Regardless, enjoy. May your taste buds be happy and your spirits bright.

Black Forest Cake Ball,
page 90

Pomegranate Spritzers,
page 36

Sweet Potato
Biscuits, page 76

holiday
feasts

This chapter is rich in swoon-worthy savories: roasts, turkeys, gravies and mashed potatoes, stuffings, vegetable dishes, and salads, all ready for a symphonic palate performance.

Moroccan Rib Roast,
page 11

Apricot-Apple Stuffed Crown Roast

Pork and fruit are a classic combo, so it just makes sense to adorn this favorite with chopped apples, apricots, and if desired, cherries.

Prep: 45 minutes **Roast:** 3¼ hours
Stand: 20 minutes **Oven:** 325°F
Makes: 12 to 16 servings

1	8- to 10-pound pork rib crown roast (12 to 16 ribs)
1	cup sliced celery
½	cup chopped onion
¼	cup butter or margarine
8	cups dry firm-textured whole wheat bread cubes
2	cups chopped apples
½	cup snipped dried apricots
½	cup dried cherries (optional)
½	teaspoon dried sage, crushed
¼	teaspoon ground black pepper
1½	cups chicken broth or water
3	tablespoons orange juice
1	tablespoon light-color corn syrup
1	teaspoon soy sauce

1. Preheat oven to 325°F. Trim fat from roast. Place crown roast, bone tips up, on a rack in a shallow roasting pan. Make a ball of foil and press it into roast cavity to hold open. Wrap the bone tips with foil. Roast for 2½ hours.

2. Meanwhile, for stuffing, in a large skillet cook celery and onion in hot butter over medium heat for 5 minutes or until tender. In a very large bowl toss together bread cubes, apples, apricots, cherries (if desired), sage, and pepper. Add broth and celery mixture. Toss gently to moisten. If desired, add enough additional broth to make a stuffing of desired moistness.

3. In a small bowl combine orange juice, corn syrup, and soy sauce; set aside.

4. Remove foil from roast cavity. Loosely pack stuffing into the center of the roast. Cover stuffing loosely with foil. Insert an oven-going meat thermometer into the center of the stuffing. Place any remaining stuffing in a lightly greased, covered casserole. Roast for 45 to 60 minutes or until thermometer in stuffing registers 165°F and the roast registers 150°F, brushing roast occasionally with the orange juice mixture. Add the stuffing in the casserole the last 45 to 60 minutes of roasting.

Apricot-Apple Stuffed Crown Roast

5. Cover crown roast with foil and let stand for 20 minutes. The temperature of the meat after standing should be 160°F. To serve, slice crown roast between the ribs. Serve the additional stuffing in casserole along with roast.

Per serving: 363 cal., 13 g total fat (5 g sat. fat), 107 mg chol., 403 mg sodium, 18 g carbo., 3 g fiber, 41 g pro.

Mustard-Rubbed Pork Roast

Three flavor partners perfect for pork—mustard, garlic, and rosemary—commingle in one awesome seasoning rub.

Prep: 15 minutes **Roast:** 1¼ hours
Stand: 15 minutes **Oven:** 325°F **Makes:** 6 servings

1	2- to 2½-pound boneless pork top loin roast (single loin)
¼	cup Dijon-style mustard
1	to 2 tablespoons bottled minced garlic
1	tablespoon snipped fresh rosemary

1. Preheat oven to 325°F. Trim fat from roast. For rub, in a small bowl combine mustard, garlic, rosemary, ½ teaspoon *salt*, and ½ teaspoon *ground black pepper*. Sprinkle rub evenly over all sides of roast; rub in with your fingers. Insert an oven-going meat thermometer near center of the roast. Place roast on a rack in a shallow roasting pan.

2. Roast for 1¼ to 1½ hours or until thermometer registers 150°F. Cover roast with foil and let stand for 15 minutes. The temperature of the meat after standing should be 160°F.

Per serving: 212 cal., 7 g total fat (2 g sat. fat), 95 mg chol., 508 mg sodium, 1 g carbo., 0 g fiber, 34 g pro.

Orchard Pork

Start to Finish: 35 minutes **Makes:** 4 servings

2	tablespoons butter or margarine
2	Bosc or Bartlett pears, cored and thinly sliced
½	cup fresh or frozen cranberries
¼	cup orange marmalade

Orchard Pork

2	teaspoons snipped fresh thyme or ½ teaspoon dried thyme, crushed
3	tablespoons packed brown sugar
½	teaspoon salt
¼	teaspoon ground black pepper
4	pork rib or loin chops, cut about 1 inch thick
1	tablespoon cooking oil
	Snipped fresh thyme (optional)

1. In a large skillet melt butter over medium heat; stir in sliced pears. Cook, stirring occasionally, for 5 minutes. Gently stir in cranberries, orange marmalade, and the 2 teaspoons thyme; heat through. Cover and keep warm.

2. Meanwhile, in a small bowl combine brown sugar, salt, and pepper. Rub both sides of chops with the brown sugar mixture.

3. In a 12-inch skillet cook chops in hot oil over medium-high heat for 10 to 12 minutes or until 160°F and juices run clear, turning once. (If chops brown too quickly, reduce heat to medium.) Top chops with warm pear mixture. If desired, garnish with additional thyme.

Per serving: 398 cal., 15 g total fat (6 g sat. fat), 87 mg chol., 409 mg sodium, 38 g carbo., 3 g fiber, 29 g pro.

Stout-Glazed Ham with
Parsnips and Onions

Spice-Rubbed Ham with Apple-Maple Sauce

*If you love the cloves-and-ham combination,
try another fragrant approach with garlic, cumin,
and mustard. Then serve it with a maple sauce
instead of a raisin or cherry sauce.*

Prep: 20 minutes **Bake:** 1½ hours **Oven:** 325°F
Makes: 8 to 10 servings

  3   tablespoons packed brown sugar
  4   teaspoons bottled minced garlic
  1   tablespoon ground cumin
  1   6- to 8-pound cooked ham (rump half or
      shank portion)
  ½   cup Dijon-style mustard
  ¼   cup apple cider
  ¼   cup pure maple syrup
      Salt and ground black pepper

1. Preheat oven to 325°F. In a small bowl combine
brown sugar, garlic, and cumin. Score ham in a
diamond pattern by making diagonal cuts at 1-inch
intervals. Rub sugar mixture evenly over ham with
your fingers. Place ham, fat side up, on a rack in a
shallow roasting pan. Insert an oven-going meat
thermometer into center of ham. (The thermometer
should not touch bone.)

2. Bake for 1½ to 2¼ hours or until thermometer
registers 140°F. Cover loosely with foil the last
30 minutes, if necessary to avoid overbrowning.

3. For sauce, in a small bowl stir together mustard,
cider, and maple syrup. Season to taste with salt
and pepper. Slice ham; serve with sauce.

Per serving: 387 cal., 8 g total fat (2 g sat. fat), 159 mg chol.,
2,293 mg sodium, 15 g carbo., 0 g fiber, 62 g pro.

Stout-Glazed Ham with Parsnips and Onions

Dip into a stash of dark Irish beer to give ham a sturdy, flavorful glaze that will cloak the crunchy parsnip-and-onion accompaniment as well.

Prep: 15 minutes **Bake:** 1½ hours **Oven:** 325°F
Makes: 6 to 8 servings

- 1   5- to 6-pound cooked ham (rump half or shank portion)
  Whole cloves
- ½   cup Irish stout (such as Guinness), apple cider, or apple juice
- ¼   cup honey
- ¼   cup butter or margarine
- 6   small parsnips, halved lengthwise
- 1   pound red boiling onions, peeled* and halved, or medium red onions, quartered

1. Preheat oven to 325°F. Score ham in a diamond pattern by making shallow diagonal cuts at 1-inch intervals; stud with cloves. Place the ham, fat side up, on a rack in a shallow roasting pan. Insert an oven-going meat thermometer into the center of the ham. (The thermometer should not touch bone.) Bake about 45 minutes or until thermometer registers 120°F.

2. Meanwhile, for glaze, in a small saucepan combine stout, honey, and butter. Bring to boiling; reduce heat. Simmer, uncovered, for 10 minutes. Set glaze aside.

3. In a small skillet cook parsnips in a small amount of boiling water for 5 minutes; drain. Arrange parsnips and onions around ham. Pour glaze over ham and vegetables. Bake for 45 to 50 minutes more or until thermometer registers 140°F and vegetables are tender, spooning pan juices over ham and vegetables once.

4. Transfer ham and vegetables to a serving platter, spooning some of the pan juices over vegetables.

Make-Ahead Directions: Prepare glaze as directed in Step 2; cool. Transfer to a covered container and chill for up to 24 hours. Before glazing the ham, transfer the glaze to a small saucepan; heat through. Pour over ham and vegetables as directed.

*Note: To peel boiling onions, cook onions in enough boiling water to cover for 30 seconds; drain. Rinse with cold water; drain again. Cool onions slightly. Cut a small slice from the root end of each onion. Squeeze from the other end to remove the onion from the peel.

Per serving: 647 cal., 17 g total fat (8 g sat. fat), 227 mg chol., 2,537 mg sodium, 47 g carbo., 7 g fiber, 79 g pro.

Moroccan Rib Roast

Coriander, cumin seeds, and crushed red pepper give this mouthwatering main dish an aromatic ethnic twist. See photo, page 7.

Prep: 20 minutes **Roast:** 1¾ hours
Stand: 15 minutes **Oven:** 350°F
Makes: 12 servings

- 2   tablespoons coriander seeds, crushed
- 2   tablespoons finely shredded lemon peel
- 1   tablespoon olive oil
- 1   teaspoon cumin seeds, crushed
- ½   to 1 teaspoon crushed red pepper
- ¼   teaspoon salt
- 1   4- to 5-pound beef rib roast
- 8   cloves garlic, slivered

1. Preheat oven to 350°F. In a small bowl stir together coriander seeds, lemon peel, oil, cumin seeds, crushed red pepper, and salt; set aside.

2. Cut ½-inch slits randomly into top and sides of roast. Insert garlic slivers deep into slits. Rub lemon mixture into surface of roast.

3. Insert an oven-going meat thermometer into center of roast. (The thermometer should not touch bone.) Place roast, fat side up, in a shallow roasting pan. Roast, uncovered, to desired doneness. Allow 1¾ to 2¼ hours for medium rare (135°F) or 2¼ to 2¾ hours for medium (150°F).

4. Cover roast with foil and let stand 15 minutes. The temperature of the meat after standing should be 145°F for medium rare or 160°F for medium.

Per serving: 163 cal., 9 g total fat (3 g sat. fat), 51 mg chol., 106 mg sodium, 1 g carbo., 1 g fiber, 17 g pro.

Cranberry
Beef Brisket

Cranberry Beef Brisket

As this hearty brisket simmers, the delicate sweetness of cranberry sauce smooths the flavor of marinara to make a tangy sauce.

Prep: 20 minutes **Cook:** 3 hours
Makes: 6 to 8 servings

1	3-pound beef brisket
	Salt and ground black pepper
1	tablespoon cooking oil
1	cup sliced celery
½	cup chopped green or red sweet pepper
½	cup chopped onion
½	cup water
1	clove garlic, minced
1	16-ounce can whole cranberry sauce
1	15- to 16-ounce can marinara sauce or tomato sauce

1. Trim fat from brisket; sprinkle with salt and pepper. Cook brisket in a 4- to 6-quart Dutch oven in hot oil about 10 minutes or until brown, turning once. Remove brisket from Dutch oven. Add celery, sweet pepper, onion, water, and garlic to Dutch oven. Cook and stir over medium heat about 5 minutes or just until vegetables are tender. Stir in the cranberry sauce and marinara sauce; cook until bubbly.

2. Return brisket to Dutch oven. Simmer, covered, about 3 hours or until tender. Remove brisket from Dutch oven; cool slightly. Boil sauce gently, uncovered, for 5 to 10 minutes or until slightly thickened. Thinly slice meat across the grain. Serve with sauce.

Per serving: 413 cal., 13 g total fat (4 g sat. fat), 76 mg chol., 549 mg sodium, 38 g carbo., 3 g fiber, 35 g pro.

Tomato-Crusted Beef Ribeye Roast

Tender, grand ribeye enjoys a new dimension with a crust of mellow-rich tomato or basil pesto brightened with mustard and lemon.

Prep: 15 minutes **Roast:** 1¾ hours
Stand: 15 minutes **Oven:** 350°F
Makes: 15 servings

1	5- to 6-pound boneless beef ribeye roast
	Salt and ground black pepper
1	6-ounce jar purchased tomato or basil pesto
1	4-ounce jar spicy coarse-grain mustard
2	teaspoons finely shredded lemon peel
2	to 4 cloves garlic, minced

1. Preheat oven to 350°F. Trim fat from roast, leaving a thin even layer of fat on the top if possible; season with salt and pepper. Insert an oven-going meat thermometer into center of roast. (The thermometer should not touch bone.) Place roast, fat side up, on a rack in a shallow roasting pan.

2. In a small bowl combine pesto, mustard, lemon peel, and garlic; set aside.

3. Roast, uncovered, to desired doneness, spreading half of the pesto mixture over top and sides of roast during the last 20 minutes of roasting. Allow 1¾ to 2 hours for medium rare (135°F) or 2 to 2½ hours for medium (150°F).

4. Cover roast and let stand for 15 minutes. The temperature of the meat after standing should be 145°F for medium rare or 160°F for medium. Serve with remaining pesto mixture.

Per serving: 289 cal., 15 g total fat (5 g sat. fat), 90 mg chol., 429 mg sodium, 2 g carbo., 1 g fiber, 31 g pro.

3. Preheat oven to 325°F. Remove turkey from brine; discard brine. Rinse turkey; pat dry with paper towels. Pull neck skin to back and secure with a small skewer. If a band of skin crosses the tail, tuck the ends of the drumsticks under the band. If there is no band of skin, tie drumsticks securely to the tail with 100-percent-cotton string. Twist wing tips under the back.

4. Place turkey, breast side up, on a rack in a shallow roasting pan. Insert an oven-going meat thermometer into the center of one of the inside thigh muscles. (The thermometer should not touch bone.) Brush turkey with oil. Cover turkey loosely with foil.

5. Roast for 2¼ hours. Remove foil; cut band of skin or string between drumsticks so thighs cook evenly. Continue roasting, uncovered, for 30 to 45 minutes more or until thermometer registers 180°F. Cover turkey with foil and let stand for 15 minutes. Carve turkey.

Per serving: 537 cal., 28 g total fat (7 g sat. fat), 203 mg chol., 995 mg sodium, 5 g carbo., 0 g fiber, 61 g pro.

Maple-Brined Turkey

Brining is a prep method in which the bird is soaked in salt water for a half day or more to produce moist, flavorful meat. Maple syrup lends a rich, sweet flavor.

Prep: 20 minutes **Roast:** 2¾ hours
Stand: 15 minutes **Marinate:** 12 hours
Oven: 325°F **Makes:** 12 servings

1½ gallons water
1½ cups maple-flavor syrup
 1 cup coarse salt
 ¾ cup packed brown sugar
 1 10-pound turkey (not self-basting)
    Cooking oil

1. For brine, in a pot large enough to hold the turkey combine water, syrup, salt, and brown sugar; stir to dissolve salt and brown sugar.

2. Rinse turkey; remove any excess fat from inside turkey. Carefully add turkey to brine. Cover and marinate in the refrigerator for 12 to 24 hours.

**Tomato-Crusted
Beef Ribeye Roast**

Roast Turkey with Sweet Onion Jam

The sweet-savory onion jam forms a crust on the bird as it roasts.

Prep: 15 minutes **Roast:** 3 hours
Stand: 15 minutes **Oven:** 325°F
Makes: 12 to 14 servings

1	10- to 12-pound turkey
	Salt (optional)
	Cooking oil
6	medium red and/or white onions, cut into wedges
10	to 12 unpeeled garlic cloves
2	tablespoons cooking oil
1	recipe Sweet Onion Jam or 1 cup purchased roasted onion jam
	Chicken broth (optional)
¼	cup dry white wine or apple juice
3	tablespoons all-purpose flour

1. Preheat oven to 325°F. Rinse turkey; pat dry with paper towels. If desired, season body cavity with salt. Pull neck skin to back and fasten with a small skewer.

2. If a band of skin crosses the tail, tuck the ends of the drumsticks under the band. If there is no band of skin, tie the drumsticks securely to the tail with 100-percent-cotton string. Twist wing tips under the back.

3. Place turkey, breast side up, on a rack in a shallow roasting pan. Insert an oven-going meat thermometer into the center of one of the inside thigh muscles. (The thermometer should not touch bone.) Brush turkey with oil. Cover turkey loosely with foil.

4. Roast turkey for 1¼ hours. Toss onion wedges and unpeeled garlic cloves with the 2 tablespoons oil. Spoon the onion mixture around the turkey and roast about 1¼ hours more or until the thermometer registers 160°F.

5. Remove foil; cut band of skin or string between drumsticks so thighs cook evenly. Carefully spread the Sweet Onion Jam over turkey. Continue roasting, uncovered, for 30 to 45 minutes more or until thermometer registers 180°F.

6. Transfer turkey, onion wedges, and garlic to a serving platter. Cover turkey with foil and let stand for 15 minutes.

7. Meanwhile, for gravy, pour pan drippings into a large measuring cup; skim fat from drippings. Strain the remaining pan drippings and add chicken broth, if necessary, to equal 1¾ cups. In a medium saucepan combine wine and flour; stir in strained pan drippings. Cook and stir over medium heat until thickened and bubbly. Cook and stir for 1 minute more. Carve turkey; serve with gravy.

Roasted Turkey with Sweet Onion Jam

Sweet Onion Jam: Cut off about ¼ inch of the pointed top of 1 whole garlic bulb so that the individual cloves show. Place the bulb, cut end up, in a custard cup. Drizzle with 1 tablespoon olive oil. Cover with foil and bake in a 325°F oven for 45 to 60 minutes or until the garlic cloves feel soft when pressed. Cool. Gently squeeze out the garlic paste from the individual cloves into a saucepan. Stir in 1 cup finely chopped sweet onion, ½ cup finely chopped Granny Smith apple, ½ cup balsamic vinegar, and ½ cup sugar. Bring to boiling over medium-high heat, stirring occasionally; reduce heat. Simmer, uncovered, about 30 minutes, stirring occasionally, until the onion and apple soften, turn transparent, and the mixture thickens. Cool. Transfer to a covered container and chill for up to 1 day. Makes about 1 cup.

Per serving: 620 cal., 29 g total fat (7 g sat. fat), 202 mg chol., 151 mg sodium, 22 g carbo., 1 g fiber, 62 g pro.

**Hazelnut-Crusted
Turkey Breast**

Hazelnut-Crusted Turkey Breast

Yes, roasting a whole bird can be overwhelming, not to mention resulting in too much meat for some. So roast a turkey breast half, all white meat with bone, instead. This version is brushed with orange marmalade and crusted with a savory nut blend.

Prep: 20 minutes **Roast:** 1½ hours
Stand: 15 minutes **Oven:** 375°F
Makes: 6 to 8 servings

- 1   **3- to 3½-pound turkey breast half with bone**
- 1   **tablespoon olive oil or cooking oil**
- 1   **clove garlic, minced**
- ¼   **teaspoon salt**
- ½   **cup hazelnuts (filberts)**
- ½   **teaspoon ground coriander**
- ¼   **teaspoon coarsely ground black pepper**
- ⅛   **teaspoon ground cinnamon**
- ¼   **cup orange marmalade**

1. Preheat oven to 375°F. Remove skin from turkey breast. Place turkey breast, bone side down, on a lightly greased rack in a shallow roasting pan. In a small bowl combine oil, garlic, and salt; brush over turkey breast. Insert an oven-going meat thermometer into the thickest portion of the breast. (The thermometer should not touch bone.) Roast turkey for 45 minutes.

2. Meanwhile, place hazelnuts in a blender or food processor. Cover and blend or process until finely chopped. Transfer nuts to a bowl; stir in coriander, pepper, and cinnamon. Set nut mixture aside.

3. Remove turkey breast from oven. Brush with orange marmalade; sprinkle with nut mixture, pressing gently so nuts stick to the turkey breast. Continue roasting, uncovered, for 45 to 60 minutes more or until thermometer registers 170°F.

4. Cover turkey breast with foil and let stand for 15 minutes. If desired, garnish with *oranges, kumquats,* and *bay leaves.*

Per serving: 260 cal., 8 g total fat (1 g sat. fat), 88 mg chol., 58 mg sodium, 9 g carbo., 1 g fiber, 38 g pro.

Pan-Seared Duck
Breasts with Apples
and Broccoli Rabe

Pan-Seared Duck Breasts with Apples and Broccoli Rabe

Simple and the epitome of elegance, duck breasts are loved for their moist, flavorful meat. Sear them before baking to melt away some fat, then serve with tart apples and bitter-crunchy broccoli rabe or kale.

Prep: 15 minutes **Bake:** 12 minutes
Cook: 15 minutes **Stand:** 10 minutes
Oven: 350°F **Makes:** 4 servings

4	7- to 8- ounce boneless duck breast halves (with skin)
	Ground black pepper
4	Golden Delicious or Gala apples, sliced
¼	cup butter or margarine
	Salt and ground black pepper
⅓	cup balsamic vinegar
¼	cup apple juice
4	cups water
4	cups broccoli rabe or kale

1. Preheat oven to 350°F. Trim excess fat from each duck breast half (do not remove skin). Score the skin side of each duck breast half at ½-inch intervals in a diamond pattern; season with pepper.

2. In a hot 12-inch ovenproof skillet cook duck breasts, skin sides down, over medium heat for 5 minutes. Turn and cook about 5 minutes more or until brown. Drain off fat. Bake duck breasts in skillet, uncovered, for 12 to 18 minutes or until an instant-read thermometer inserted into duck registers 155°F. Remove duck from skillet, reserving 1 tablespoon drippings in skillet. Cover with foil; let stand 10 minutes (the temperature of the duck will rise 5°F during standing).

3. Meanwhile, in a large skillet cook apples in hot butter over medium heat about 10 minutes or until tender, stirring frequently. Season apples to taste with salt and pepper; keep warm.

4. For sauce, add vinegar and apple juice to reserved drippings in skillet, scraping up crusty browned bits. Bring to boiling over medium-high heat. Boil gently for 3 to 5 minutes or until liquid is reduced by half.

5. In a large saucepan bring water to boiling; add broccoli rabe. Cook for 1 minute; drain. To serve, arrange duck breast halves, broccoli rabe, and apples on a serving platter; drizzle with sauce.

Per serving: 484 cal., 20 g total fat (10 g sat. fat), 183 mg chol., 414 mg sodium, 29 g carbo., 6 g fiber, 44 g pro.

Loaded Oyster Stew

Start to Finish: 40 minutes
Makes: 8 appetizer servings or 6 main-dish servings

1	8-ounce package sliced fresh mushrooms
½	cup finely chopped onion
½	cup chopped celery
½	cup chopped red sweet pepper
2	tablespoons butter or margarine
2	tablespoons all-purpose flour
¼	teaspoon white pepper
2	cups milk
1	cup shredded sharp cheddar cheese
1	10¾-ounce can condensed cream of potato soup
1	pint shucked oysters, undrained

1. In a 4-quart Dutch oven cook and stir mushrooms, onion, celery, and sweet pepper in hot butter until tender. Stir in flour and pepper. Stir in milk all at once. Cook and stir over medium heat until thickened and bubbly.

2. Stir cheese and potato soup into Dutch oven. Cook and stir until cheese melts. Stir in undrained oysters. Cook for 5 to 8 minutes more or until oysters curl around the edges, stirring occasionally.

Per serving: 185 cal., 11 g total fat (6 g sat. fat), 52 mg chol., 489 mg sodium, 12 g carbo., 1 g fiber, 10 g pro.

Barley Waldorf Salad

Maybe you or your mom enjoyed this classic at the tearoom of your Gram's favorite department store. Build on tradition with this healthy, zesty salad update with nutty barley, fresh grapes, and a tangy yogurt dressing.

Prep: 25 minutes   **Cook:** 45 minutes
Stand: 30 minutes   **Chill:** up to 24 hours
Makes: 6 to 8 servings

¾	cup regular barley
3¾	cups water
1¼	teaspoons salt
¼	cup plain yogurt
3	tablespoons mayonnaise or salad dressing
¼	teaspoon finely shredded lemon peel
1	tablespoon lemon juice
¼	teaspoon sugar
1½	cups seedless green and/or red grapes, halved
1	cup chopped apple
½	cup chopped celery
	Milk
¼	cup coarsely chopped walnuts, toasted*

1. In a large skillet toast barley over medium-low heat for 4 to 5 minutes or until barley is golden, stirring occasionally. In a 3-quart saucepan combine toasted barley, water, and ½ teaspoon of the salt. Bring to boiling; reduce heat to medium-low. Simmer, covered, about 45 minutes or until barley is tender; drain. Let barley stand for 30 minutes to cool.

2. Whisk together yogurt, mayonnaise, lemon peel, lemon juice, sugar, and the remaining ¾ teaspoon salt. Stir in cooked barley, grapes, apple, and celery. Cover and chill for up to 24 hours.

3. To serve, stir a little milk into salad to moisten, if necessary. Sprinkle with walnuts.

*Note: To toast nuts, spread them in a single layer in a shallow baking pan. Bake in a preheated 350°F oven for 5 to 10 minutes or until pieces are golden brown, stirring once or twice. Cool completely.

Per serving: 202 cal., 10 g total fat (1 g sat. fat), 5 mg chol., 548 mg sodium, 27 g carbo., 5 g fiber, 5 g pro.

Chopped Holiday Salad

If you are of Italian heritage, you know antipasto, a beautifully composed platter of savory tidbits. This attractive salad is along the antipasto lines, combining chopped veggies dressed in a light olive oil, herb, and cheese dressing.

Prep: 30 minutes **Chill:** 2 hours
Makes: 8 to 10 servings

1   15- to 19-ounce can cannellini beans (white kidney beans), rinsed and drained
2   small green sweet peppers, cut into bite-size chunks (1½ cups)
1   medium cucumber, cut into bite-size chunks (3 cups)
½   head radicchio or ¼ head red cabbage, coarsely chopped (2 cups)
½   of a 16-ounce package radishes, halved or quartered (1½ cups)
¼   cup olive oil
¼   cup lemon juice
    Honey (about 1 tablespoon)
    Coarse salt (about ½ teaspoon)
    Cracked black pepper (about ¼ teaspoon)
8   ounces feta cheese, cubed
    Coarsely chopped fresh Italian (flat-leaf) parsley

1. In separate resealable plastic bags, place beans, sweet pepper, cucumber, radicchio, and radishes.

2. For dressing, in a screw-top jar combine oil and lemon juice. Cover; shake well. Add honey, salt, and pepper to taste. Cover; shake well. Pour 1 to 2 tablespoons of the dressing into each bag; seal bags. Chill 2 to 4 hours, turning bags occasionally.

3. To serve, transfer vegetables with dressing to a large salad bowl. Add feta cheese; toss gently to combine. Sprinkle with parsley.

Per serving: 191 cal., 13 g total fat (5 g sat. fat), 25 mg chol., 534 mg sodium, 15 g carbo., 3 g fiber, 8 g pro.

Holiday Slaw

This is no ordinary slaw as the only standard ingredient is shredded cabbage. Transform it by tossing in oranges, wine, honey, anise, fennel, apple, and crunchy cucumber. It's beautiful served from a glass compote on a brunch buffet.

Prep: 50 minutes **Chill:** 2 hours
Makes: 12 servings

2   teaspoons finely shredded blood orange peel or orange peel
⅔   cup blood orange juice or orange juice
½   cup salad oil
2   tablespoons white wine vinegar
2   tablespoons honey
1   teaspoon anise seeds, crushed
¼   teaspoon salt
2   medium fennel bulbs
3   red apples, cored and cut into thin wedges
2   tablespoons lemon juice
6   cups shredded green or red cabbage
5   blood oranges or oranges, peeled and thinly sliced
4   cups thinly sliced cucumber

1. For dressing, in a screw-top jar combine orange peel, orange juice, oil, vinegar, honey, anise seeds, and salt. Cover and shake well. Set dressing aside.

2. Cut off and discard upper stalks of fennel bulbs. Remove any wilted outer layers; cut a thin slice from the base of each fennel bulb. Wash bulbs; cut each bulb into thin slices. In a medium bowl toss together apple wedges and lemon juice.

3. To assemble salad, line a serving platter with shredded cabbage. Arrange the orange slices, cucumber slices, fennel slices, and apple wedges on the cabbage-lined platter. Pour half of the dressing over salad. Cover and chill for up to 2 hours. Cover and chill remaining dressing. Just before serving, shake remaining dressing well; pour over salad.

Make-Ahead Directions: Prepare dressing as directed in Step 1. Cover and chill for up to 3 days. Shake well before using.

Per serving: 164 cal., 9 g total fat (1 g sat. fat), 0 mg chol., 68 mg sodium, 21 g carbo., 4 g fiber, 2 g pro.

Spinach and
Sweet Red Onion Salad

This holiday, wilt greens with a hot red wine and grenadine syrup for a refreshing twist on the classic hot bacon and vinegar version.

Start to Finish: 25 minutes **Makes:** 6 servings

1   large red onion, halved lengthwise and
    sliced (about 1½ cups)
1   tablespoon butter
½   cup dry red wine
2   tablespoons grenadine syrup or
    boysenberry syrup
1   tablespoon sugar
⅛   teaspoon salt
1   5- to 6-ounce package fresh baby spinach
    (8 cups)
    Salt and ground black pepper

1. For onion topping, in a large nonstick skillet cook onion in hot butter over medium-high heat for 5 to 8 minutes or until tender, stirring occasionally. Stir in wine, grenadine syrup, sugar, and salt. Bring to boiling; reduce heat. Boil gently, uncovered, for 10 to 12 minutes or until most of the liquid evaporates and the remaining liquid is like syrup.

2. Meanwhile, place spinach in a large salad bowl. Spoon onion topping over spinach; toss gently to combine. Season to taste with salt and pepper. Serve immediately.

Make-Ahead Directions: Prepare onion topping as directed in Step 1; cool. Cover; chill in an airtight container up to 4 hours. Reheat and spoon topping over spinach; toss gently to combine.

Per serving: 77 cal., 2 g total fat (1 g sat. fat), 5 mg chol., 182 mg sodium, 11 g carbo., 1 g fiber, 1 g pro.

Chopped
Holiday Salad

Cranberry-Pear
Gelatin Salads

New Cranberry Sauce

The flavors of persimmon and pomegranate add a sweet-sour tang to this beautiful holiday standard.

Prep: 10 minutes **Cook:** 20 minutes
Makes: 12 servings

1	cup chopped onion
2	cloves garlic, minced
1	tablespoon olive oil or cooking oil
1	12-ounce bag fresh or frozen cranberries
1	cup pomegranate juice or cranberry juice
¾	cup sugar
½	teaspoon ground ginger
1	medium fuyu persimmon or apple, cored and cut into ¼-inch cubes
	Fresh rosemary sprig (optional)

1. In large saucepan cook onion and garlic in hot oil over medium-high heat for 2 to 3 minutes or until onions begin to soften. Stir in cranberries, pomegranate juice, sugar, and ginger. Bring to boiling; reduce heat to medium-low. Simmer, uncovered, stirring occasionally, for 16 to 17 minutes, or until mixture is just thickened. Remove saucepan from heat; stir in persimmon. Serve warm, at room temperature, or cover and chill up to 48 hours. If desired, garnish with rosemary sprig.

Per serving: 91 cal., 1 g total fat (0 g sat. fat), 0 mg chol., 2 mg sodium, 21 g carbo., 2 g fiber, 0 g pro.

Cranberry-Pear Gelatin Salads

Prep: 20 minutes **Chill:** 5 hours
Makes: 10 to 12 servings

½	cup sugar
2	envelopes unflavored gelatin
2½	cups cranberry juice
1	cup carbonated water
2	medium pears, peeled, cored, and chopped
½	cup dried cranberries
30	to 36 sugared cranberries (optional)

1. In a medium saucepan stir together the sugar and gelatin. Stir in ½ cup of the cranberry juice. Cook and stir over medium heat until sugar and gelatin dissolve. Remove saucepan from heat. Stir in the remaining 2 cups cranberry juice and carbonated water.

2. Transfer gelatin mixture to a large bowl; cover and chill for 1 to 2 hours or until slightly thickened. Stir in pears and dried cranberries. Divide gelatin mixture between ten to twelve 5- to 6-ounce individual molds or custard cups. (Or pour gelatin mixture into a 2-quart baking dish.) Cover and chill for 4 to 24 hours or until firm.

3. Remove gelatin from molds, if using. If desired, garnish each salad with sugared cranberries.

Per serving: 176 cal., 0 g total fat (0 g sat. fat), 0 mg chol., 81 mg sodium, 44 g carbo., 1 g fiber, 1 g pro.

Cranberry-Grape Sauce

Transform a traditional cranberry relish into a sweet mixture with the addition of plump and juicy red grapes and a cup of wine.

Prep: 15 minutes **Cook:** 25 minutes
Makes: 12 servings

1	cup white Zinfandel wine or white grape juice
1	cup sugar
¼	cup water
1	12-ounce package cranberries
1½	cups seedless red grapes, halved
1	teaspoon grated fresh ginger
⅛	teaspoon ground cloves

1. In a large saucepan combine wine, sugar, and water. Bring to boiling, stirring occasionally until sugar dissolves. Add cranberries, grapes, ginger, and cloves. Return to boiling; reduce heat. Cook, covered, for 15 minutes, stirring occasionally. Uncover and cook for 10 to 15 minutes more or until desired consistency, stirring occasionally. Serve warm, at room temperature, or cover and chill for up to 3 days.

Per serving: 107 cal., 0 g total fat (0 g sat. fat), 0 mg chol., 2 mg sodium, 24 g carbo., 1 g fiber, 0 g pro.

Brandy-Cream Gravy with Roasted Garlic

If your annual gravy becomes a bit same-old, same-old, wake it up with brandy and roasted garlic to accompany roast turkey or chicken.

Prep: 15 minutes **Bake:** 1 hour **Cook:** 1 hour
Oven: 325°F **Makes:** 2½ cups

- 1 **large whole garlic bulb**
- 1 **teaspoon olive oil**
- 1 **turkey gizzard**
- 1 **turkey neck, halved**
- 2 **cups water**
    Pan drippings from roasted turkey or chicken
- ¼ **cup all-purpose flour**
- ⅓ **cup whipping cream**
- 2 **tablespoons brandy**
- 1 **teaspoon lemon juice**
- ½ **teaspoon snipped fresh thyme**
    Salt and ground black pepper

1. Preheat oven to 325°F. Cut off and discard ¼ inch of the pointed top of the garlic bulb to expose the individual cloves. Leaving bulb whole, remove any loose, papery outer layers. Place the garlic bulb, cut end up, in a custard cup; drizzle with olive oil. Cover with foil and bake about 1 hour or until the cloves feel soft when pressed. Set aside just until cool enough to handle. Squeeze out the garlic paste from individual cloves; set garlic paste aside.

2. For giblet broth, rinse gizzard and neck. In a medium saucepan combine water, gizzard, and neck. Bring to boiling; reduce heat. Simmer, covered, about 1 hour or until tender. Discard gizzard and neck. Line a colander or sieve with two layers of 100-percent-cotton cheesecloth. Set colander in a heatproof bowl; carefully pour giblet broth into lined colander. Set broth aside.

3. Pour pan drippings from turkey or chicken into a fat separator or a large glass measuring cup. If using a fat separator, pour off fat into a glass measuring cup. (If using a large measuring cup, use a spoon to skim and reserve fat from drippings.) Pour ¼ cup of the fat into a medium saucepan; discard remaining fat. Add enough of the giblet broth to the pan drippings to equal 1⅔ cups.

4. Stir flour into fat in saucepan. Stir pan drippings, whipping cream, and brandy all at once into flour mixture in saucepan. Cook and stir over medium heat until thickened and bubbly. Cook and stir for 1 minute more. Stir in the roasted garlic paste, lemon juice, and thyme. Season to taste with salt and pepper; heat through.

Per ¼ cup: 135 cal., 10 g total fat (4 g sat. fat), 48 mg chol., 45 mg sodium, 4 g carbo., 0 g fiber, 6 g pro.

New Cranberry Sauce

Savory Squash Pilaf

There is rice pilaf and wild rice pilaf. Now there is fragrant squash pilaf comprised of winter squash cubes, rice, raisins, allspice, and parsley.

Start to Finish: 35 minutes **Makes:** 4 to 6 servings

⅓	cup finely chopped onion
1	tablespoon walnut oil or cooking oil
⅔	cup uncooked long grain rice
3	tablespoons golden raisins
¼	teaspoon ground allspice
1⅓	cups reduced-sodium chicken broth
1½	cups peeled, seeded, and cubed winter squash (such as acorn, butternut, or buttercup)
2	teaspoons snipped fresh Italian (flat-leaf) parsley
	Fresh Italian (flat-leaf) parsley

1. In a medium saucepan cook and stir onion in hot oil over medium heat about 4 minutes or just until tender. Stir in rice, raisins, and allspice. Carefully stir in broth. Bring to boiling; reduce heat. Simmer, covered, for 5 minutes. Stir in squash cubes.

Cook for 10 to 12 minutes more or until rice is tender but still firm and squash is just tender. Remove saucepan from heat; stir in snipped parsley. If desired, garnish with additional parsley.

Per serving: 189 cal., 4 g total fat (0 g sat. fat), 0 mg chol., 211 mg sodium, 35 g carbo., 1 g fiber, 4 g pro.

Apple-Pecan Wild Rice Pilaf

Prep: 10 minutes **Cook:** 30 minutes
Makes: 6 servings

1	cup finely chopped onion
1	cup sliced celery
1	tablespoon butter or margarine
1	cup apple juice
1	6-ounce package long grain and wild rice mix
¼	teaspoon ground cinnamon
1	cup chopped red apple
½	cup chopped pecans, toasted (see Note, page 17)

1. In a large saucepan cook onion and celery in hot butter until tender. Stir in apple juice and 1 cup *water*; bring to boiling. Stir in wild rice mix, seasoning packet, and cinnamon; reduce heat. Simmer, covered, about 30 minutes or until rice is tender. Remove saucepan from heat. Gently stir in apple and pecans.

Per serving: 217 cal., 9 g total fat (2 g sat. fat), 5 mg chol., 431 mg sodium, 33 g carbo., 3 g fiber, 4 g pro.

Brown Bread Stuffing

Rich, velvety brown bread—yes, fresh from the can—makes a luscious dressing along with squash, celery, sage, and a host of aromatic herbs and spices. Try it with prime rib or beef tenderloin.

Prep: 35 minutes **Bake:** 45 minutes **Oven:** 325°F
Makes: 10 to 12 servings

7	cups honey wheat bread cubes
1	16-ounce can brown bread with raisins, cut into ½-inch cubes (5 cups)
6	tablespoons butter or margarine

Savory
Squash Pilaf

Apple-Pecan
Wild Rice Pilaf

4   **cups peeled, seeded winter squash (such as butternut or acorn), cut into ¾-inch cubes**
1½   **cups coarsely chopped celery**
1   **large red onion, cut into thin wedges**
2¼   **to 2¾ cups chicken broth**
¼   **cup snipped fresh sage or 2 teaspoons dried sage, crushed**
2   **tablespoons snipped fresh Italian (flat-leaf) parsley**
1   **teaspoon ground nutmeg**

1. Preheat oven to 325°F. Spread bread cubes in 2 shallow baking pans. Melt 4 tablespoons of the butter; drizzle over bread cubes, tossing to coat. Bake, uncovered, for 15 to 20 minutes or until lightly toasted, stirring once. Transfer to a very large bowl.

2. Meanwhile, melt the remaining 2 tablespoons butter in a 12-inch skillet over medium heat. Add squash cubes. Cook, uncovered, for 5 minutes, stirring occasionally. Add celery and onion.

Cook, covered, for 10 minutes more. Stir in ¼ cup of the chicken broth. Cook, covered, about 5 minutes more or until squash is just tender, stirring occasionally. Remove skillet from heat; stir in sage, parsley, nutmeg, ½ teaspoon *salt*, and ½ teaspoon *ground black pepper*.

3. Add squash mixture to bread in bowl. Add 2 cups of the remaining broth, tossing lightly to coat. Add enough additional broth to make a stuffing of desired moistness.

4. Transfer stuffing to a greased 3-quart casserole. Bake, covered, for 30 minutes. Uncover; bake for 15 to 20 minutes more or until heated through.

Make-Ahead Directions: Prepare toasted bread cubes as directed in Step 1. Store in an airtight container at room temperature for up to 2 days.

Per serving: 264 cal., 8 g total fat (4 g sat. fat), 19 mg chol., 806 mg sodium, 44 g carbo., 5 g fiber, 7 g pro.

Cranberry-Apple
Corn Bread Stuffing

Cranberry-Apple Corn Bread Stuffing

*Typical corn bread stuffing is embellished with
sausage. To lighten and brighten the stuffing,
substitute crunchy apples and dried tart cranberries.*

Prep: 35 minutes **Bake:** 50 minutes **Oven:** 325°F
Makes: 12 to 14 servings

1½	cups chopped celery
1	cup chopped onion
½	cup butter or margarine
6	cups crumbled corn bread or corn bread stuffing mix
6	cups dry white or whole wheat bread cubes
2	cups chopped unpeeled Granny Smith apples
1	cup dried cranberries or cherries
2	tablespoons snipped fresh sage or 1½ teaspoons dried sage, crushed
1	tablespoon snipped fresh thyme or 1 teaspoon dried thyme, crushed
½	teaspoon salt
½	teaspoon ground black pepper
1¾	to 2 cups chicken broth (if using stuffing mix, use 3 to 3¼ cups broth)

1. Preheat oven to 325°F. In a large Dutch oven
cook and stir celery and onion in hot butter about
5 minutes or until tender; remove from heat.
Stir corn bread, bread cubes, apples, cranberries,
sage, thyme, salt, and pepper into onion mixture.
Add enough broth to make stuffing of desired
moistness, tossing lightly to combine.

2. Transfer the stuffing to a 3-quart rectangular
baking dish. Bake, covered, for 35 minutes.
Uncover and bake for 15 to 20 minutes more
or until heated through.

Per serving: 293 cal., 14 g total fat (7 g sat. fat), 49 mg chol.,
648 mg sodium, 37 g carbo., 3 g fiber, 5 g pro.

Wild Rice with Wild Mushrooms

Prep: 20 minutes Cook: 30 minutes
Makes: 6 servings

- 4 cups fresh cremini or button mushrooms, sliced
- ½ cup chopped onion
- 1 clove garlic, minced
- 1 tablespoon olive oil
- 2 cups water
- 2 tablespoons dry white wine
- 1 6-ounce package long grain and wild rice mix
- ½ teaspoon dried sage, crushed
- ¼ cup snipped fresh parsley
- ¼ cup chopped walnuts, toasted (see Note, page 17)

1. In a large saucepan cook mushrooms, onion, and garlic in hot oil until tender. Stir in water and wine; bring to boiling. Stir in rice mix, seasoning packet, and sage; reduce heat. Simmer, covered, for 30 to 35 minutes or until rice is tender and liquid is absorbed. Remove saucepan from heat; stir in parsley and walnuts.

Per serving: 172 cal., 6 g total fat (1 g sat. fat), 0 mg chol., 408 mg sodium, 26 g carbo., 2 g fiber, 5 g pro.

Tomato-Mushroom Corn Pudding

This recipe surpasses your everyday corn pudding, luscious as it may be. It kicks up the flavor and texture with earthy dried porcini mushrooms, dried tomatoes, English muffin toast, and Parmesan cheese.

Prep: 20 minutes Bake: 45 minutes
Stand: 10 minutes Chill: 4 hours Oven: 375°F
Makes: 6 servings

- ¼ cup dried porcini mushrooms
- 3 to 6 dried tomatoes
- 4 cups torn, lightly toasted English muffins (about 4 muffins) or dry bread cubes
- 1½ cups frozen whole kernel corn, thawed
- ½ cup finely shredded Parmesan cheese
- 1 tablespoon snipped fresh basil or 1 teaspoon dried basil, crushed
- ½ teaspoon salt
- ¼ teaspoon coarsely ground black pepper
- 4 eggs, lightly beaten
- 1½ cups milk

1. Place porcini mushrooms and tomatoes in separate small bowls. Cover both mushrooms and tomatoes with boiling water. Soak for 15 minutes; drain well. Rinse mushrooms; drain again, pressing out excess moisture. Chop dried tomatoes.

2. In a 2-quart square baking dish toss together English muffins, mushrooms, tomatoes, corn, Parmesan cheese, basil, salt, and pepper. In a medium bowl beat eggs and milk with a wire whisk or rotary beater until combined. Pour egg mixture evenly over mixture in baking dish. Cover and chill for at least 4 hours or up to 24 hours.

3. Preheat oven to 375°F. Bake, uncovered, about 45 minutes or until a knife inserted in center comes out clean. Let stand for 10 minutes before serving.

Per serving: 261 cal., 10 g total fat (4 g sat. fat), 150 mg chol., 520 mg sodium, 31 g carbo., 3 g fiber, 13 g pro.

Tomato-Mushroom
Corn Pudding

Honey-Glazed Carrots

This is an update on the buttered variety, jazzed up with lemon peel and crushed red pepper.

Start to Finish: 30 minutes **Makes:** 12 servings

- 6   cups water
- 3   pounds packaged peeled baby carrots
- 3   to 4 tablespoons honey
- 2   tablespoons butter or margarine
- 1   teaspoon finely shredded lemon peel
- ½   teaspoon crushed red pepper
- ½   teaspoon salt
-     Crushed red pepper (optional)

1. In a very large heavy skillet bring water to boiling; add carrots. Return to boiling; reduce heat. Simmer, covered, for 8 to 10 minutes or until just tender. Drain; pat dry with paper towels.

2. For glaze, in the same skillet combine honey, butter, lemon peel, crushed red pepper, and salt. Stir constantly over medium heat until butter melts and mixture bubbles. Carefully add carrots. Toss gently for 2 to 3 minutes or until carrots are thoroughly coated with glaze and heated through.

3. To serve, transfer the carrots to a shallow bowl or serving platter. Drizzle with remaining glaze from skillet. If desired, sprinkle with additional crushed red pepper.

Per serving: 75 cal., 2 g total fat (1 g sat. fat), 5 mg chol., 180 mg sodium, 14 g carbo., 3 g fiber, 1 g pro.

Orange-Glazed Pearl Onions

Fans of creamed onions will enjoy this simple, special onion dish. Pretty pearl onions are glazed in marmalade and seasonings.

Start to Finish: 40 minutes **Makes:** 4 to 6 servings

- 1   pound unpeeled pearl onions
- 1   clove garlic, thinly sliced
- 1   tablespoon cooking oil
- ½   cup orange marmalade
- ½   teaspoon salt
- ⅛   teaspoon ground black pepper
- 1   tablespoon snipped fresh chives or parsley

1. In a medium saucepan cook onions in enough boiling water to cover for 1 minute; drain. Cool onions slightly; carefully remove skins. In the same saucepan cook onions, covered, in a small amount of boiling lightly salted water for 10 minutes or until tender; drain and set aside.

2. In a large skillet cook and stir garlic in hot oil over medium-high heat about 30 seconds or until golden. Stir in marmalade until melted. Stir in cooked onions, salt, and pepper. Cook and stir for 3 to 5 minutes or until marmalade is slightly thickened and onions are coated. Stir in chives.

Per serving: 173 cal., 3 g total fat (1 g sat. fat), 0 mg chol., 316 mg sodium, 37 g carbo., 2 g fiber, 1 g pro.

Orange-Glazed
Pearl Onions

Green Bean Casserole with Crispy Shallots

Give this standard holiday buffet dish new life. Start by skipping the canned beans in favor of fresh beans and a silky sauce of cream, Parmesan cheese, olive oil, and seasonings finished with a crunchy topping of crisp-fried shallots.

Prep: 45 minutes **Bake:** 20 minutes **Oven:** 375°F
Makes: 8 servings

- 1½ pounds haricots verts or thin green beans, trimmed
- 12 ounces fresh button mushrooms, sliced
- 12 ounces fresh shiitake mushrooms, stems discarded and caps sliced
- 2 tablespoons bottled minced garlic
- 1 tablespoon snipped fresh thyme or 1 teaspoon dried thyme, crushed
- ¼ cup butter or margarine
- ¼ teaspoon salt
- ¼ teaspoon ground black pepper
- 2 tablespoons all-purpose flour
- 2 cups half-and-half or light cream
- ½ cup finely shredded Parmesan cheese
- ⅓ cup pine nuts, toasted (See note, page 17)
- ½ cup olive oil
- 4 large shallots, thinly sliced crosswise, or 1 cup thinly sliced sweet onion

Green Bean Casserole with Crispy Shallots

1. Preheat oven to 375°F. Lightly grease a 2-quart casserole; set aside. In a 12-inch skillet cook the beans, uncovered, in boiling lightly salted water about 3 minutes or until crisp-tender; drain. Transfer the beans to a bowl of ice water to stop cooking; drain again.

2. In the same skillet cook button and shiitake mushrooms, garlic, and thyme in 2 tablespoons of the hot butter over medium-high heat until mushrooms are tender and excess liquid has evaporated. Stir in the ¼ teaspoon salt and the ¼ teaspoon pepper. Gently toss mushroom mixture with beans.

3. For sauce, in a small saucepan melt the remaining 2 tablespoons butter over medium heat. Stir in flour. Stir in half-and-half all at once. Cook and stir over medium heat until thickened and bubbly. Cook and stir 1 minute more. Stir in the Parmesan cheese, ⅛ teaspoon *salt*, and ⅛ teaspoon

ground black pepper. Pour sauce over green bean mixture, stirring gently until just combined. Transfer green bean mixture to prepared casserole.

4. Bake, uncovered, about 20 minutes or until hot and bubbly. Sprinkle with pine nuts.

5. Meanwhile, in another small saucepan heat oil over medium-high heat. Fry shallots, in small batches, about 1½ minutes or until golden brown and slightly crisp. Using a slotted spoon, transfer shallots to paper towels to drain. Just before serving, top casserole with fried shallots.

Make-Ahead Directions: Prepare as directed through Step 3. Cover and chill for up to 24 hours. Fry shallots as directed in Step 5; drain and transfer to a covered container. Chill for up to 24 hours. To serve, let casserole stand at room temperature for 30 minutes before baking as directed in Step 4. Top casserole with fried shallots.

Per serving: 385 cal., 32 g total fat (11 g sat. fat), 41 mg chol., 270 mg sodium, 21 g carbo., 4 g fiber, 9 g pro.

Mustard-Glazed
Brussels Sprouts
and Oranges

Mustard-Glazed Brussels Sprouts and Oranges

These crunchy "little cabbages" are sumptuous in a butter sauce, but ever so luscious cloaked in this sweet, mustard-citrus glaze.

Start to Finish: 25 minutes **Makes:** 5 or 6 servings

- 3 medium blood oranges and/or oranges
- 1 pound Brussels sprouts (about 4 cups)
- 1 tablespoon butter or margarine
- 2 teaspoons cornstarch
- ¼ teaspoon five-spice powder or dried dill
- 2 tablespoons honey mustard

1. Finely shred enough peel from 1 of the oranges to make ½ teaspoon peel; set peel aside. Halve the orange; squeeze juice. Working over a bowl to catch the juices, peel and section the remaining 2 oranges; set orange sections aside. Combine the juices to make ⅓ cup, adding water if necessary. Set juice aside.

2. Trim stems and remove any wilted outer leaves from Brussels sprouts; wash. Halve any large sprouts. In a medium saucepan cook sprouts, uncovered, in a small amount of boiling water for 10 to 12 minutes or until tender. Drain; transfer to a serving bowl. Gently stir in the orange sections; cover and keep warm.

3. In the same saucepan melt butter. Stir in cornstarch and five-spice powder. Stir in reserved orange peel, orange juice, and mustard. Cook and stir until thickened and bubbly. Cook and stir for 1 minute more. Spoon over Brussels sprouts and orange sections; toss gently to coat.

Per serving: 102 cal., 3 g total fat (2 g sat. fat), 6 mg chol., 73 mg sodium, 19 g carbo., 5 g fiber, 4 g pro.

Orange-Sauced Broccoli

Do you love a saucy broccoli? Skip the familiar hollandaise or white sauce and give this whipping cream version a try. Spike it with orange juice concentrate and cracked black pepper for extra flavor.

Start to Finish: 25 minutes **Makes:** 10 to 12 servings

3 cups water
¾ teaspoon salt
12 cups broccoli florets and/or broccoli rabe, cut into 1½-inch pieces
1 cup whipping cream
1 tablespoon frozen orange juice concentrate, thawed
½ teaspoon cracked black pepper
⅓ cup sliced almonds, toasted (see Note, page 17)

1. In a 4-quart Dutch oven bring water and salt to boiling; add broccoli. Return to boiling; reduce heat. Simmer, covered, for 8 to 10 minutes or until crisp-tender. Drain; transfer to a serving bowl.

2. Stir whipping cream into Dutch oven. Bring to boiling. Boil gently, uncovered, about 3 minutes or until thickened, stirring occasionally. Stir in orange juice concentrate and pepper. Spoon over broccoli; sprinkle with almonds.

Per serving: 141 cal., 11 g total fat (6 g sat. fat), 33 mg chol., 162 mg sodium, 9 g carbo., 3 g fiber, 4 g pro.

Cauliflower Crowns with Pesto and Prosciutto

Are you looking for lighter, healthier fare to bring to the table? Try this crunchy cauliflower with a light dressing of nuts, parsley, and tarragon, spiked with prosciutto.

Start to Finish: 30 minutes **Makes:** 12 servings

2 heads cauliflower (about 1½ pounds each)
1 cup snipped fresh parsley
½ cup smoked walnuts or almonds
½ cup olive oil
2 tablespoons snipped fresh tarragon or 2 teaspoons dried tarragon, crushed
2 cloves garlic
1 teaspoon red wine vinegar
2 tablespoons butter or margarine, melted
2 tablespoons finely chopped prosciutto or crisp-cooked, crumbled bacon

1. Wash cauliflower heads; remove leaves and woody stems. Break each cauliflower head into 6 to 8 clusters. In a 6-quart Dutch oven cook cauliflower, covered, in a small amount of boiling salted water for 8 to 10 minutes or until crisp-tender; drain. Arrange cauliflower clusters in a large shallow serving dish; cover and keep warm.

2. Meanwhile, for pesto, in a food processor or blender combine parsley, walnuts, oil, tarragon, garlic, and vinegar. Cover and process or blend with several on-off turns until smooth.

3. Drizzle cauliflower with the melted butter; sprinkle with prosciutto. Spoon pesto into a small bowl; serve with cauliflower.

Make-Ahead Directions: Prepare pesto as directed in Step 2. Cover and chill for up to 2 days. About 30 minutes before serving, let pesto come to room temperature. Continue as directed.

Per serving: 155 cal., 15 g total fat (3 g sat. fat), 5 mg chol., 69 mg sodium, 5 g carbo., 2 g fiber, 3 g pro.

Cauliflower Crowns with Pesto and Prosciutto

Mashed Potatoes with Garden Confetti

Confetti is a visual cue to celebrate. Do so by tossing a bright, crunchy blend of cooked carrots, celery, and onion on top of soft, creamy potatoes.

Prep: 20 minutes **Cook:** 20 minutes
Makes: 10 to 12 servings

5	pounds red potatoes (about 15 medium), unpeeled and quartered
1½	teaspoons salt
1	8-ounce package cream cheese, cut up and softened
1	to 1¼ cups half-and-half or light cream
1	teaspoon salt
1	teaspoon cracked black pepper
	Salt and cracked black pepper
1	recipe Garden Confetti
2	tablespoons butter or margarine, melted

1. In a 6-quart Dutch oven cook potatoes and the 1½ teaspoons salt, covered, in enough boiling water to cover for 20 to 25 minutes or until tender; drain.

2. Mash potatoes with a potato masher or beat with an electric mixer on low speed until slightly lumpy. Add cream cheese, half-and-half, the 1 teaspoon salt, and 1 teaspoon pepper. Beat until combined. Season to taste with additional salt and pepper.

3. Transfer potatoes to a serving bowl. Spoon Garden Confetti over potatoes; drizzle with the melted butter.

Garden Confetti: In a large skillet melt 2 tablespoons butter or margarine over medium heat. Add 2 medium carrots, shredded; 1 stalk celery, finely chopped; and 1 medium onion, thinly sliced. Cook and stir for 4 to 5 minutes or until vegetables are tender. Keep warm until needed.

Per serving: 336 cal., 16 g total fat (10 g sat. fat), 46 mg chol., 484 mg sodium, 44 g carbo., 4 g fiber, 7 g pro.

Festive Mashed Potatoes

Snow pea pods, roasted red sweet peppers, and cheese are unexpected but colorful in this mashed potato version, built on a convenience product.

Prep: 20 minutes **Bake:** 30 minutes **Oven:** 350°F
Makes: 6 to 8 servings

1	cup fresh or frozen snow pea pods
1	24-ounce package (about 3 cups) refrigerated home-style mashed potatoes
½	of an 8-ounce tub cream cheese spread with chive and onion, softened
¼	cup milk
	Dash ground black pepper
1	cup shredded mozzarella or Monterey Jack cheese
½	cup bottled roasted red sweet peppers, drained and coarsely chopped
2	tablespoons grated Parmesan cheese

1. Preheat oven to 350°F. Lightly grease a 2-quart baking dish; set aside. In a small saucepan cook pea pods in a small amount of boiling water for 3 to 4 minutes or just until tender; drain. Cut pea pods in half crosswise; set aside.

2. In a large bowl stir together mashed potatoes, cream cheese, milk, and black pepper. Gently stir in shredded cheese, sweet peppers, and pea pods. Transfer to prepared baking dish. Sprinkle with Parmesan cheese. Bake, uncovered, about 30 minutes or until heated through.

Per serving: 227 cal., 11 g total fat (7 g sat. fat), 33 mg chol., 400 mg sodium, 20 g carbo., 2 g fiber, 9 g pro.

Sour Cream and Chive
Mashed Potatoes

Sour Cream and Chive Mashed Potatoes

Here is a sublime recipe for a beloved holiday standard: mashers. Ahhhh, yum.

Prep: 15 minutes **Cook:** 20 minutes
Makes: 8 to 10 servings

 1   5-pound bag baking potatoes (such as russet or Yukon gold), peeled, if desired, and quartered
 1   tablespoon salt
 1   8-ounce carton dairy sour cream
 ⅓   cup butter or margarine
 ½   teaspoon salt
 ¼   teaspoon ground black pepper
 ½   to ¾ cup milk
 ¼   cup snipped fresh chives
     Snipped fresh chives (optional)

1. In a 6-quart Dutch oven cook potatoes and the 1 tablespoon salt, covered, in enough boiling water to cover for 20 to 25 minutes or until tender; drain.

2. Mash with a potato masher or beat with an electric mixer on low speed. Add sour cream, butter, the ½ teaspoon salt, and pepper. Gradually beat in enough of the milk to make mixture light and fluffy. Just before serving, stir in the ¼ cup chives. If desired, sprinkle with additional chives.

Per serving: 355 cal., 14 g total fat (9 g sat. fat), 34 mg chol., 529 mg sodium, 52 g carbo., 6 g fiber, 7 g pro.

Sweet Potato Bake
with Streusel Topping

Sweet Potato Bake with Streusel Topping

Start with prepared, refrigerated mashed sweet potatoes to cut the preparation time. This gently spiced, nutty sweet-top treatment delivers 100 percent flavor and texture.

Prep: 25 minutes **Bake:** 40 minutes
Stand: 5 minutes **Oven:** 350°F **Makes:** 8 servings

1   24-ounce package refrigerated mashed sweet potatoes (about 3 cups)
2   eggs, lightly beaten
½   cup light cream, half-and-half, or milk
1   cup apple pie filling
½   cup packed brown sugar
⅓   cup all-purpose flour
⅓   cup rolled oats
¼   cup butter
½   cup chopped walnuts or pecans

1. Preheat oven to 350°F. Lightly grease a 2-quart baking dish; set aside. In a large bowl combine sweet potatoes, eggs, and light cream. Coarsely chop any large pieces of apple in the apple pie filling; stir into sweet potato mixture. Transfer to prepared baking dish.

2. For topping, in a medium bowl combine brown sugar, flour, and oats. Using a pastry blender, cut in butter until the pieces are pea-size. Stir in nuts. Sprinkle evenly over sweet potato mixture.

3. Bake, uncovered, for 40 to 45 minutes or until center is just set and topping is light brown. Let stand 5 minutes before serving.

Per serving: 314 cal., 14 g total fat (6 g sat. fat), 74 mg chol., 155 mg sodium, 43 g carbo., 3 g fiber, 5 g pro.

Glazed Sweet Potatoes

Are you weary of marshmallow-topped sweet potatoes? Try this casserole turned tart and snappy with maple syrup, mustard, and cranberries.

Prep: 20 minutes **Bake:** 1 hour **Oven:** 325°F
Makes: 8 servings

2	pounds sweet potatoes (4 to 5 medium)
⅓	cup pure maple syrup or maple-flavor syrup
3	tablespoons coarse-grain Dijon-style mustard
2	tablespoons cooking oil
½	teaspoon salt
¼	to ½ teaspoon ground black pepper
½	cup fresh or frozen cranberries

1. Preheat oven to 325°F. Peel sweet potatoes; cut into 1½-inch chunks. In a large bowl combine maple syrup, mustard, oil, salt, and pepper. Add sweet potato chunks and cranberries; toss to coat. Transfer to a 3-quart rectangular baking pan.

2. Bake, covered, for 50 to 60 minutes or until sweet potatoes are tender; stir gently. Bake, uncovered, for 10 to 15 minutes more or until sweet potatoes are glazed. Stir before serving.

Per serving: 144 cal., 3 g total fat (0 g sat. fat), 00 mg chol., 324 mg sodium, 26 g carbo., 3 g fiber, 1 g pro.

Chipotle Scalloped Sweet Potatoes

Scalloped potatoes, loved for their soft and crusty texture, take a Southwestern turn with the choice of sweet spuds, Mexican cheese, and chipotle peppers in adobo sauce. Serve with a simple meat, such as ham.

Prep: 35 minutes **Bake:** 40 minutes
Stand: 10 minutes **Oven:** 350°F
Makes: 8 to 10 servings

2½	pounds sweet potatoes (about 3 large), peeled and thinly sliced
½	cup chopped onion
2	tablespoons butter or margarine
2	tablespoons all-purpose flour
½	teaspoon salt
1½	cups milk
1½	teaspoons finely chopped canned chipotle peppers in adobo sauce
6	ounces queso quesadilla, queso blanco, or Monterey Jack cheese, shredded (1½ cups)

1. Preheat oven to 350°F. In a 4-quart Dutch oven cook sweet potato slices in lightly salted boiling water for 5 minutes; drain and set aside. Grease a 2-quart rectangular baking dish; set aside.

2. For sauce, in a small saucepan cook onion in hot butter about 5 minutes or until tender. Stir in flour and salt. Add milk all at once; stir in chipotle pepper. Cook and stir over medium heat until thickened and bubbly. Remove saucepan from heat; stir in cheese.

3. Place half of the sweet potato slices in the prepared baking dish. Cover with half of the sauce. Repeat the layers.

4. Bake, covered, for 25 minutes. Uncover and bake about 15 minutes more or until potatoes are tender. Let stand for 10 minutes before serving.

Per serving: 169 cal., 6 g total fat (3 g sat. fat), 19 mg chol., 324 mg sodium, 24 g carbo., 3 g fiber, 6 g pro.

appetizer
spread

If you plan an appetizer buffet,
contribute to one, or just want
to set out a little something to
eat before leaving for a show,
this is your chapter. From
cheese balls and chicken wings
to elegant olives and punches,
you will find them all, each
in tempting new variations.

Spicy Taco Cheese Log,
page 41

Pomegranate Spritzers

The sweet-tart flavor of pomegranate and its ruby red hue make a refreshing and attractive mixer using fruity white wine and sparkling water.

Start to Finish: 15 minutes **Makes:** 8 servings

- 1   cup pomegranate-flavor syrup for flavoring coffee
- 1   750-milliliter bottle fruity white wine (such as Riesling or Chardonnay), chilled
- 1   cup sparkling water, chilled
     Ice cubes (optional)
     Pomegranate seeds (optional)
     Blood orange wedges (optional)

1. Place 2 tablespoons pomegranate-flavor syrup in each of eight champagne flutes. In a 1½- to 2-quart pitcher combine the wine and sparkling water. Slowly pour wine mixture into each glass. If desired, add ice cubes to glasses. If desired, garnish each serving with pomegranate seeds and/or a blood orange wedge.

Per serving: 180 cal., 0 g total fat (0 g sat. fat), 0 mg chol., 31 mg sodium, 30 g carbo., 0 g fiber, 0 g pro.

Tea and Cider Wassail

Cider, beer, and wine are the base of this traditional English hot, spicy punch. Reworked without the alcohol, the punch blends hot tea and four fruit juices for a luscious drink to enjoy until the bowl is empty. For a group, serve the punch from a slow cooker to keep it warm.

Prep: 15 minutes **Cook:** 30 minutes
Makes: about twenty-two (8-ounce) servings

- 6   cups freshly brewed hot tea
- 6   cups cranberry juice
- 6   cups apple cider or apple juice
- 3   cups orange juice
- 1½ cups sugar
- 1¼ cups lemon juice
- 1   9-inch piece stick cinnamon, broken
- ¾   teaspoon whole cloves
     Apple slices (optional)

1. In a 6- to 8-quart Dutch oven combine tea, cranberry juice, apple cider, orange juice, sugar, and lemon juice. For spice bag, place cinnamon and cloves in the center of a double-thick, 6-inch square of 100-percent-cotton cheesecloth. Bring the corners together and tie with clean kitchen string. Add spice bag to Dutch oven.

2. Bring mixture to boiling, stirring until sugar dissolves; reduce heat. Simmer, covered, for 30 minutes. Remove spice bag; discard. If desired, garnish each serving with an apple slice.

Slow cooker directions: In a 6-quart slow cooker combine all ingredients. Cover and cook on low-heat setting for 5 to 6 hours or on high-heat setting for 2½ to 3 hours. Remove spice bag; discard. Keep warm on low-heat setting for up to 2 hours.

Per serving: 139 cal., 0 g total fat (0 g sat. fat), 0 mg chol., 4 mg sodium, 35 g carbo., 0 g fiber, 0 g pro.

Cosmo Fruit Punch

Do you love fancy drinks but detest the work of making individual cocktails? Serve Cosmopolitans in a punch! Set citrus twists in a tiny bowl alongside the glasses.

Start to Finish: 15 minutes
Makes: fourteen (6-ounce) servings

- 4   cups cranberry juice, chilled
- ½   of a 12-ounce can frozen limeade concentrate, thawed
- 4   cups lemon-lime carbonated beverage, chilled
- 2   cups orange vodka or vodka
- ⅓   cup orange liqueur
     Ice cubes
     Orange twists and/or slices (optional)
     Lime twists and/or slices (optional)

1. In a large pitcher or punch bowl stir together cranberry juice and limeade concentrate. Slowly pour carbonated beverage down side of pitcher. Gently stir in vodka and orange liqueur. Serve over ice cubes. If desired, garnish each serving with orange and/or lime twists.

Per serving: 180 cal., 0 g total fat (0 g sat. fat), 0 mg chol., 17 mg sodium, 26 g carbo., 0 g fiber, 0 g pro.

Pomegranate Spritzers

Eggnog Punch

Softened French vanilla or cinnamon ice cream teams with zippy cream soda and eggnog for an uncommon holiday punch. Serve it with candy canes or cinnamon sticks.

Start to Finish: 15 minutes
Makes: about twenty-four (6-ounce) servings

1¾ to 2 quarts French vanilla or cinnamon ice cream
2 quarts dairy eggnog or canned eggnog, chilled
1 1-liter bottle cream soda, chilled
Peppermint sticks or candy canes
Ground cinnamon

1. Place ice cream in an extra large punch bowl; add half the eggnog. Use a potato masher to gently stir and mash ice cream mixture until ice cream melts and mixture is combined. Stir in the remaining eggnog. Slowly pour in cream soda, stirring to combine. Sprinkle each serving with cinnamon; serve with peppermint sticks.

Per serving: 224 cal., 11 g total fat (7 g sat. fat), 79 mg chol., 77 mg sodium, 26 g carbo., 0 g fiber, 5 g pro.

Minty Cocoa

Butter mints melt into hot, sweet cocoa for kid-loving flavor.

Start to Finish: 10 minutes **Makes:** 8 to 10 servings

8 cups water
2½ cups instant cocoa mix
½ cup butter mints, crushed
Whipped cream (optional)
Unsweetened cocoa powder (optional)
Peppermint sticks or candy canes

1. In a large saucepan heat water until hot but not boiling. Whisk in cocoa mix and butter mints until mints melt and mixture is combined. If desired, top each serving with whipped cream and sprinkle with cocoa powder. Serve with peppermint sticks.

Per serving: 177 cal., 2 g total fat (1 g sat. fat), 1 mg chol., 98 mg sodium, 38 g carbo., 0 g fiber, 1 g pro.

Hot Buttered Rum Batter

Spiced ice cream in a mug of hot rum is a perfect holiday drink.

Start to Finish: 20 minutes
Makes: about 16 servings (3⅓ cups batter)

1 cup butter, softened
1 cup packed brown sugar
2 cups powdered sugar
1 teaspoon ground cinnamon
½ teaspoon ground nutmeg
½ teaspoon ground cloves
1 pint vanilla ice cream, softened
1 cup dark rum

Eggnog Punch

Hot Buttered Rum Batter

Boiling water
Cinnamon sticks (optional)
Ground nutmeg (optional)

1. In a large mixing bowl beat butter with an electric mixer on medium to high speed for 30 seconds. Add brown sugar and beat until combined. Beat in powdered sugar, cinnamon, the ½ teaspoon nutmeg, and cloves. Beat in ice cream until nearly smooth (mixture still will have small lumps). Place batter in a covered airtight container and freeze for up to 1 month (batter will not freeze solid).

2. For each serving, spoon about 3 tablespoons batter and 1 tablespoon rum into an 8- to 10-ounce heatproof mug; add ¾ cup boiling water. If desired, serve with stick cinnamon and sprinkle with additional nutmeg.

Per serving: 282 cal., 14 g total fat (9 g sat. fat), 38 mg chol., 101 mg sodium, 33 g carbo., 0 g fiber, 1 g pro.

Hot Buttered Cider: Prepare as above, except omit rum and substitute hot apple cider for the boiling water.

39

¼ cup butter or margarine, melted
1½ teaspoons dried sage, crushed
1 cup chocolate-covered raisins

1. Preheat oven to 300°F. In a large shallow roasting pan combine the crackers, sweet potato sticks, peanuts, and corn. Combine the melted butter and sage; drizzle over cracker mixture. Stir until well coated.

2. Bake, uncovered, for 20 to 25 minutes or until lightly toasted, stirring twice. Spread on a large piece of foil to cool. When cool, stir in the raisins. Store in a covered airtight container for up to 2 weeks.

Per ½ cup: 199 cal., 11 g total fat (3 g sat. fat), 5 mg chol., 145 mg sodium, 21 g carbo., 2 g fiber, 5 g pro.

Roasted Tomatillo
and Jalapeño
Guacamole

Roasted Tomatillo and Jalapeño Guacamole

Start with an ordinary container of purchased guacamole. To it, add roasted vegetables, cumin, garlic, and lime for anything but ordinary flavor.

Prep: 15 minutes **Roast:** 20 minutes **Oven:** 450°F
Makes: 16 servings

12 ounces tomatillos, husked, rinsed, and halved or one 11-ounce can whole tomatillos, drained, rinsed, and halved
6 fresh jalapeño chile peppers, halved and seeded (see Note, page 58)
1 medium onion, sliced
2 tablespoons cooking oil
1 teaspoon ground cumin
2 cloves garlic, minced
1 teaspoon finely shredded lime peel
1 tablespoon lime juice
1 16-ounce carton refrigerated guacamole
2 tablespoons pumpkin seeds or sliced almonds, toasted (see Note, page 17)
Vegetable dippers (such as jicama strips; green, yellow, and/or red sweet pepper strips; or packaged peeled baby carrots) and/or tortilla chips

1. Preheat oven to 450°F. Arrange tomatillos and chile peppers, cut sides down, in a shallow baking pan; add onion slices. In a small bowl combine oil,

Trail Mix

Here's a fresh new blend to pack in little bags and take to the sledding hill or skating rink: whole grain crackers, sweet potato sticks, peanuts, and corn are roasted and drizzled with sage-infused butter, then tossed with raisins.

Prep: 15 minutes **Bake:** 20 minutes **Cool:** 1 hour
Oven: 300°F **Makes:** about 13 cups

1 9- to 9½-ounce package ranch-flavored whole grain crackers
1 5-ounce package southwestern-spiced sweet potato sticks or 3 cups shoestring potatoes
1 12-ounce can (2⅓ cups) honey-roasted peanuts
1 3-ounce package freeze-dried roasted sweet corn or one 4-ounce container freeze-dried whole kernel corn

cumin, and garlic; brush over vegetables. Roast, uncovered, about 20 minutes or until lightly charred; cool.

2. Chop the roasted vegetables; drain off any liquid. Stir lime peel and lime juice into guacamole. Transfer guacamole mixture to a serving bowl; top with chopped vegetables. Sprinkle with pumpkin seeds. Serve with vegetable dippers and/or tortilla chips.

Make-Ahead Directions: Prepare roasted vegetables as directed in Step 1. Cover and chill for up to 24 hours. Continue as directed.

Per serving: 69 cal., 6 g total fat (1 g sat. fat), 1 mg chol., 71 mg sodium, 4 g carbo., 1 g fiber, 1 g pro.

Spicy Taco Cheese Log

Mixing your own cheese ball is much more fun than purchasing one from a mall shop or kiosk. This one blends taco cheese, jalapeño chile peppers, and crushed corn chips.

Prep: 35 minutes **Stand:** 15 minutes **Chill:** 4 hours
Makes: 32 servings

1	8-ounce package cream cheese
1	cup shredded taco cheese
¼	cup butter or margarine
1	tablespoon milk
½	teaspoon Worcestershire sauce for chicken
2	tablespoons thinly sliced green onion
2	tablespoons bottled chopped green jalapeño chile peppers (see Note, page 58)
½	cup crushed corn chips
1	tablespoon snipped fresh cilantro
1	recipe Baked Tortilla Chips

1. In a large mixing bowl let cream cheese, taco cheese, and butter stand at room temperature for 30 minutes. Add milk and Worcestershire sauce. Beat with an electric mixer on medium speed until light and fluffy. Stir in green onion and chile peppers. Cover and chill for 4 to 24 hours.

2. Shape cheese mixture into a log about 9 inches long. Combine corn chips and cilantro; roll cheese log in corn chip mixture. Let stand for 15 minutes before serving. Serve with Baked Tortilla Chips.

Baked Tortilla Chips: Preheat oven to 350°F. Lightly coat a baking sheet with nonstick cooking spray; set aside. Lightly coat both sides of four 8-inch flour tortillas with nonstick cooking spray. Cut each tortilla into 8 wedges; sprinkle lightly with salt. Arrange wedges in a single layer on baking sheet. Bake for 12 to 15 minutes or until crisp and light brown.

Per 1 tablespoon: 75 cal., 4 g total fat (3 g sat. fat), 15 mg chol., 118 mg sodium, 4 g carbo., 0 g fiber, 1 g pro.

Spicy Taco Cheese Log

Fruited Cheese Logs

Three rich and luscious fruits flavor a soft, mellow cheese blend that is rolled in toasted almonds.

Prep: 30 minutes **Stand:** 30 minutes **Chill:** 4 hours
Makes: 32 servings

- ½   cup snipped dried apricots
- ⅓   cup snipped golden raisins
- ¼   cup snipped pitted whole dates
- 2   cups shredded Monterey Jack cheese
- ½   of an 8-ounce package cream cheese
- 2   tablespoons orange juice
- ¼   teaspoon salt
- ½   cup chopped almonds, toasted
       (see Note, page 17)
       Assorted crackers and/or apple slices

1. In a small bowl soak apricots, raisins, and dates in enough hot water to cover about 30 minutes or until softened. Drain well; set aside. Meanwhile, place Monterey Jack cheese and cream cheese in a medium mixing bowl. Let stand at room temperature for 30 minutes.

2. Add orange juice to cheeses in bowl. Beat with an electric mixer until well combined. Stir in drained apricots, raisins, dates, and salt. Divide cheese mixture in half.

3. Shape one portion of the cheese mixture into a log about 5 inches long. Repeat with remaining cheese mixture. Cover and chill logs for 4 to 24 hours. Before serving, roll each log in nuts. Serve with assorted crackers and/or apple slices.

Per 1 tablespoon: 61 cal., 4 g total fat (2 g sat. fat), 10 mg chol., 67 mg sodium, 4 g carbo., 1 g fiber, 2 g pro.

Marinated Cheese

Snappy seasonings, lemon juice, and aromatic shredded lemon peel impart terrific flavor to cheese cubes.

Prep: 20 minutes **Stand:** 1 hour **Chill:** 3 days
Makes: 12 to 16 servings

- 1   pound Monterey Jack or provolone cheese,
       cut into ¾-inch cubes
- ½   cup extra-virgin olive oil

- 1½   teaspoons finely shredded lemon peel
- ¼   cup lemon juice
- 1½   teaspoons dried whole mixed peppercorns,
       cracked, or ½ teaspoon ground
       black pepper
- 1   teaspoon fennel, cumin, or mustard
       seeds, crushed
- 3   cloves garlic, minced

1. Place cheese cubes in a resealable plastic bag. For marinade, in a screw-top jar combine oil, lemon peel, lemon juice, peppercorns, fennel seeds, and garlic. Cover and shake well. Pour over cheese in bag. Seal bag; turn to coat. Chill for up to 3 days, turning bag occasionally.

2. Let cheese stand at room temperature for 1 hour before serving. Transfer cheese cubes and marinade to a serving bowl.

Per serving: 224 cal., 20 g total fat (8 g sat. fat), 34 mg chol., 203 mg sodium, 1 g carbo., 0 g fiber, 10 g pro.

Chipotle-Cheddar Cheesecake with Chunky Salsa

Cheese balls are fabled holiday fare. This version is baked in a springform pan.

Prep: 50 minutes **Bake:** 32 minutes **Stand:** 1 hour
Chill: 4 hours **Oven:** 375°F **Makes:** 16 servings

- 4   8-inch flour tortillas
- 3   tablespoons butter or margarine, melted
- 2   8-ounce packages cream cheese, softened
- 1   cup finely shredded cheddar cheese
- ¼   cup milk
- 1   canned chipotle pepper in adobo sauce,
       drained and finely chopped
- ½   teaspoon dried oregano, crushed
- 2   eggs, lightly beaten
- 1   recipe Chunky Salsa
- 1   recipe Chipotle Chips

1. Preheat oven to 375°F. Place tortillas on a baking sheet. Bake for 12 to 14 minutes or until golden brown; cool. Cut tortillas into pieces; transfer to a food processor or blender. Cover and process or blend until finely ground. Measure 1 cup of the tortilla crumbs; discard any remaining crumbs.

**Chipotle-Cheddar
Cheesecake
with Chunky Salsa**

2. In a small bowl combine the 1 cup crumbs and melted butter. Press crumb mixture onto the bottom of a greased 9-inch springform pan; set aside.

3. For filling, in a large mixing bowl beat cream cheese, cheddar cheese, milk, chipotle pepper, and oregano with an electric mixer until well combined. Stir in eggs just until combined. Carefully spread filling evenly into crust-lined pan. Bake about 20 minutes or until center is just set.

4. Cool in pan on a wire rack for 15 minutes. Loosen crust from sides of pan; cool for 30 minutes. Remove sides of pan; cool completely on a wire rack. Cover and chill for at least 4 hours or up to 48 hours.

5. Let cheesecake stand at room temperature for 1 hour before serving. Using a slotted spoon, spread the Chunky Salsa over the cheesecake. Serve with Chipotle Chips.

Chunky Salsa: In a bowl combine 4 plum tomatoes, seeded and chopped; ⅓ cup chopped red onion; 2 green onions, thinly sliced; 2 tablespoons snipped fresh cilantro or parsley; 1 clove garlic, minced; 1 tablespoon lime juice; ¼ teaspoon salt; and ⅛ teaspoon ground black pepper.

Chipotle Chips: Preheat oven to 375°F. In a small bowl combine ¼ cup cooking oil and 1 to 2 teaspoons drained and finely chopped canned chipotle peppers in adobo sauce; brush over one side of eight 8-inch flour tortillas. Cut each tortilla into 8 wedges. Arrange wedges in a single layer on baking sheets. Bake for 12 to 14 minutes or until light brown. Transfer to a wire rack and let cool.

Make-Ahead Directions: Prepare Chunky Salsa; cover and chill for up to 24 hours. Prepare Chipotle Chips; store in an airtight container for up to 3 days.

Per serving: 263 cal., 20 g total fat (10 g sat. fat), 71 mg chol., 289 mg sodium, 14 g carbo., 1 g fiber, 7 g pro.

Caraway Veggies

Instead of serving veggies and a cheese spread, provide marinated veggies with plenty of crunch and flavor all their own.

Prep: 45 minutes **Chill:** 2 hours
Makes: 12 servings

1½	pounds small carrots with tops, trimmed and peeled, or 12 ounces packaged peeled fresh baby carrots
6	cups cauliflower florets
2	medium red and/or green sweet peppers, cut into wedges
¾	cup salad oil
1	tablespoon caraway seeds, crushed
1	cup white wine vinegar
½	teaspoon salt
½	teaspoon crushed red pepper

1. In a medium saucepan cook carrots, covered, in a small amount of boiling water for 3 to 5 minutes or until crisp-tender. Drain; rinse with cold water. Drain well. In a large saucepan cook cauliflower, covered, in a small amount of boiling water about 3 minutes or until crisp-tender. Drain; rinse with cold water. Drain well. Place carrots, cauliflower, and sweet pepper in separate resealable plastic bags.

2. For marinade, in a small saucepan combine oil and caraway seeds. Cook and stir over low heat for 4 to 5 minutes or until oil is warm and slightly fragrant; cool slightly. In a large glass measure whisk together the oil mixture, vinegar, salt, and crushed red pepper.

3. Pour about ½ cup of the marinade over the carrots, about 1 cup of the marinade over the cauliflower, and the remaining marinade over the sweet pepper. Seal bags; turn to coat. Chill for 2 to 6 hours, turning bags often.

4. To serve, drain vegetables, discarding marinade. Arrange vegetables on a serving platter.

Per serving: 85 cal., 5 g total fat (1 g sat. fat), 0 mg chol., 85 mg sodium, 9 g carbo., 3 g fiber, 2 g pro.

Caraway Veggies

Herb-Baked Olives

Marinating and baking olives in a wine-based herb marinade infuses them with satisfying flavor.

Prep: 15 minutes **Bake:** 45 minutes **Chill:** 2 hours
Oven: 375°F **Makes:** 6 servings

1½	cups mixed imported Greek and/or Italian olives
½	cup dry white wine
¼	cup olive oil
2	4-inch sprigs fresh rosemary
1	tablespoon finely shredded orange peel
2	tablespoons orange juice
1	tablespoon snipped fresh rosemary
1	tablespoon snipped fresh parsley
⅛	teaspoon ground black pepper
3	cloves garlic, minced

1. Preheat oven to 375°F. In a 15×10×1-inch baking pan combine olives, wine, 1 tablespoon of the olive oil, and the rosemary sprigs. Bake 45 to

60 minutes or until most of the liquid is absorbed, stirring occasionally. Discard rosemary sprigs.

2. Meanwhile, for marinade, in a small bowl combine the remaining 3 tablespoons olive oil, orange peel, orange juice, snipped rosemary, parsley, pepper, and garlic.

3. Pour marinade over olive mixture; toss gently to coat. Transfer olive mixture to an airtight container. Cover and chill at least 2 hours or up to 1 week.

Per ¼ cup: 155 cal., 14 g total fat (1 g sat. fat), 0 mg chol., 377 mg sodium, 4g carbo., 2 g fiber, 0 g pro.

Deviled Eggs

Has a plate of deviled eggs ever returned home with leftovers? No way. Nor will it when filled with Italian, Greek, Indian, or Mexican flavor variations.

Start to Finish: 30 minutes **Makes:** 12 servings

- 7 hard-cooked eggs, peeled
- ¼ cup mayonnaise or salad dressing
- 1 to 2 teaspoons Dijon-style mustard or honey mustard
- ½ teaspoon dry mustard
  Salt and ground black pepper
  Paprika

1. Using a sharp knife, halve 6 of the hard-cooked eggs lengthwise; remove yolks. Set whites aside. Coarsely chop the remaining hard-cooked egg.

2. In a heavy resealable plastic bag combine the egg yolks, chopped egg, mayonnaise, mustard, and dry mustard. Seal bag; gently squeeze to combine ingredients. Season to taste with salt and pepper.

3. Cut a small hole in one corner of the bag. Squeeze bag, pushing egg yolk mixture through hole into egg white halves. Sprinkle with paprika. Cover and chill until serving time (up to 24 hours).

Per serving: 72 cal., 6 g total fat (1 g sat. fat), 109 mg chol., 62 mg sodium, 0 g carbo., 0 g fiber, 3 g pro.

Italian-Style Deviled Eggs: Prepare as above, except omit mayonnaise, both mustards, and paprika. Add ¼ cup bottled creamy Italian salad dressing

Deviled Eggs, Italian-Style Deviled Eggs, Mexican-Style Deviled Eggs

and 2 tablespoons shredded Parmesan cheese to yolk mixture. Top with additional shredded Parmesan cheese and small fresh basil leaves.

Greek-Style Deviled Eggs: Prepare as at left, except add 2 tablespoons crumbled feta cheese, 1 tablespoon finely chopped pitted kalamata olives, and 2 teaspoons snipped fresh oregano to yolk mixture.

Mexican-Style Deviled Eggs: Prepare as at left, except omit mayonnaise, both mustards, and paprika. Add 3 tablespoons dairy sour cream, 1 tablespoon bottled salsa, and ½ teaspoon ground cumin to yolk mixture. Top with additional salsa and small fresh cilantro leaves.

Indian-Style Deviled Eggs: Prepare as at left, except omit mayonnaise, both mustards, and paprika. Add 3 tablespoons plain low-fat yogurt, 1 tablespoon chopped chutney, and ½ teaspoon curry powder to yolk mixture. Sprinkle with chopped peanuts.

Tapenade
Spirals

3. To serve, slice each tortilla roll into seven slices; arrange on a serving platter. If desired, garnish with parsley.

Per spiral: 68 cal., 4 g total fat (2 g sat. fat), 5 mg chol., 137 mg sodium, 7 g carbo., 1 g fiber, 1 g pro.

Panzanella Bruschetta

Traditional panzanella, a bread salad, combines pieces of bread with veggies, herbs, and dressing. The bread and salad notion translates here to savory pita chips topped with shredded greens and a Mediterranean mix of chopped veggies and seasonings.

Prep: 25 minutes **Stand:** 15 minutes
Makes: about 30 servings

1½	cups shredded baby salad greens
8	small red and/or yellow cherry or pear-shape tomatoes, quartered, or ½ cup chopped seeded tomato
¼	cup finely shredded Parmesan cheese
¼	cup chopped seeded cucumber
2	tablespoons finely chopped red onion
2	tablespoons snipped fresh basil
1	tablespoon capers, rinsed and drained
1	small clove garlic, minced
2	teaspoons red wine vinegar
2	teaspoons olive oil
	Dash salt and ground black pepper
1	recipe Baked Pita Chips

Tapenade Spirals

The French make a lovely relish of finely chopped olives and herbs called tapenade. Mix it with cream cheese, spread on tortillas, then roll, chill, and slice to expose the spiral. They are as pretty as they are bursting with flavor.

Prep: 20 minutes **Chill:** 1 hour **Makes:** 21 spirals

1	cup pitted ripe or Greek black olives, drained
1	tablespoon olive oil or cooking oil
2	teaspoons capers, drained
2	teaspoons lemon juice or lime juice
3	9- to 10-inch flour tortillas
½	of an 8-ounce tub cream cheese spread with chive and onion
	Lettuce leaves
1	cup roasted red sweet peppers, well drained and cut into thin strips
	Fresh Italian (flat-leaf) parsley sprigs (optional)

1. In a food processor combine olives, oil, capers, and lemon juice. Cover and process with several on-off turns until olives are very finely chopped.

2. Arrange tortillas on a flat surface. Spread one-third of the cream cheese spread over each tortilla; top each with one-third of the olive mixture. Place several lettuce leaves on top of the olive mixture. Arrange one-third of the sweet pepper strips over lettuce on each tortilla. Roll up tortillas; wrap in plastic wrap. Chill for 1 to 4 hours.

Panzanella Bruschetta

1. In a medium bowl combine salad greens, tomatoes, Parmesan cheese, cucumber, onion, basil, capers, and garlic. Sprinkle with vinegar, oil, salt, and pepper; toss gently to coat. Let stand for 15 to 30 minutes for flavors to blend. To serve, top Baked Pita Chips with the greens mixture.

Baked Pita Chips: Preheat oven to 350°F. Split three large pita bread rounds in half horizontally. Lightly coat the rough sides of each pita bread half with nonstick cooking spray; sprinkle each half with ½ to ¾ teaspoon onion powder, garlic powder, or ground black pepper. Cut each half into six wedges. Arrange wedges in a single layer on baking sheets. Bake for 10 to 12 minutes or until crisp; cool on wire racks.

Make-Ahead Directions: Prepare Baked Pita Chips; store in an airtight container for up to 1 week or freeze for up to 3 months. Thaw chips, covered, at room temperature.

Per serving: 24 cal., 1 g total fat (0 g sat. fat), 0 mg chol., 58 mg sodium, 4 g carbo., 0 g fiber, 1 g pro.

Cheddar-Jelly Thumbprints

Cheddar-Jelly Thumbprints

Thumbprint cookies and their traditional jam filling are always popular. Try this spunky savory version with red and/or green jalapeño jelly topping a cheddar cheese cookie.

Prep: 30 minutes **Bake:** 15 minutes per batch
Oven: 350°F **Makes:** about 42 appetizers

1½	cups shredded white cheddar cheese or extra sharp cheddar cheese
½	cup finely shredded Parmesan cheese
½	cup butter, softened
1	egg yolk
¼	teaspoon ground black pepper
1	cup all-purpose flour
1	egg white
1	tablespoon water
1¼	cups finely chopped pecans
⅓	to ½ cup green and/or red jalapeño jelly

1. Preheat oven to 350°F. Lightly grease 2 large baking sheets or line with parchment paper; set aside. In a food processor combine cheddar cheese, Parmesan cheese, and butter. Cover and process until combined. Add egg yolk and pepper; process until combined. Add flour. Process with on/off turns until a soft dough forms; set aside. (Or in a large mixing bowl beat butter with an electric mixer for 30 seconds. Beat in cheeses until combined. Beat in egg yolk and pepper until combined. Add flour; beat until soft dough forms.)

2. In a small bowl combine egg white and water. Shape dough into ¾-inch balls. Roll balls in egg-white mixture, then in pecans. Place 1 inch apart on prepared baking sheets. Press your thumb into the center of each ball.

3. Bake about 15 minutes or until edges are firm and light brown. Press puffed centers down using the rounded side of a measuring teaspoon. Transfer to a wire rack and let cool. Just before serving, fill centers with jelly.

Make-Ahead Directions: Prepare and bake as directed. Cover and chill unfilled thumbprints in an airtight container for up to 3 days or freeze for up to 3 months. Thaw in container at room temperature before filling with jelly.

Per appetizer: 81 cal., 6 g total fat (2 g sat. fat), 16 mg chol., 60 mg sodium, 4 g carbo., 0 g fiber, 0 g pro.

Sensational Stuffed Portobellos

Stuffed mushrooms, usually prepared with smaller button funghi, take on a meatier, earthier style when prepared with large portobellos. Italian cheese and pesto studded with chopped peppers and nuts fill the mushroom halves. There is plenty to savor.

Prep: 20 minutes **Broil:** 5 minutes
Makes: 12 appetizers

6	4- to 5-inch fresh portobello mushroom caps
¾	cup bottled roasted red sweet peppers, drained and cut into strips
¼	cup purchased basil pesto
1½	ounces sliced pepperoni, coarsely chopped
⅓	cup walnuts, toasted and chopped (see Note, page 17)
⅛	to ¼ teaspoon crushed red pepper
1	cup shredded Italian cheese blend

1. Preheat broiler. Remove stems and gills from mushroom caps. Arrange mushroom caps, stemmed sides up, in an ungreased shallow baking pan. Broil 3 to 4 inches from the heat for 4 minutes.

2. Meanwhile, for filling, in a medium bowl combine sweet peppers, pesto, pepperoni, walnuts, and crushed red pepper. Spoon filling evenly into mushroom caps; sprinkle with cheese. Broil for 1 to 2 minutes more or until filling is heated through. To serve, cut each mushroom cap in half.

Per appetizer: 132 cal., 11 g total fat (2 g sat. fat), 12 mg chol., 166 mg sodium, 5 g carbo., 1 g fiber, 7 g pro.

Chipotle Chicken Meatballs

Cocktail meatballs are always a hit at holiday gatherings. This variation heads to the Southwest for its inspiration of chipotle peppers and chili sauce.

Prep: 30 minutes **Bake:** 10 minutes
Cook: 10 minutes **Oven:** 350°F **Makes:** 48 meatballs

	Nonstick cooking spray
1	egg, lightly beaten
¼	cup fine dry bread crumbs
¼	cup finely chopped onion
1	tablespoon finely chopped canned chipotle peppers in adobo sauce
¼	teaspoon salt
2	cloves garlic, minced
1	pound uncooked ground chicken or turkey
½	of a 16-ounce can jellied cranberry sauce
1	cup bottled chili sauce
1	to 2 tablespoons finely chopped canned chipotle peppers in adobo sauce

1. Preheat oven to 350°F. Lightly coat a 15×10×1-inch baking pan with cooking spray; set aside. For meatballs, in a large bowl combine egg, bread crumbs, onion, 1 tablespoon chipotle peppers, salt, and garlic. Add ground chicken; mix well. Shape chicken mixture into 48 meatballs.

2. Arrange meatballs in a single layer in prepared pan. Bake, uncovered, for 10 to 15 minutes or until no longer pink (165°F). Drain well.

3. Meanwhile, for sauce, in a large skillet stir together cranberry sauce, chili sauce, and the 1 to 2 tablespoons chipotle peppers. Cook and stir over medium heat until cranberry sauce melts.

4. Add cooked meatballs to sauce. Cook, uncovered, about 10 minutes or until heated through, stirring occasionally. Serve immediately or keep warm in a slow cooker on low-heat setting.

Make-Ahead Directions: Prepare meatballs as directed in Step 1. Cover and chill unbaked meatballs for up to 24 hours. Continue as directed.

Per meatball: 31 cal., 1 g total fat (0 g sat. fat), 13 mg chol., 104 mg sodium, 4 g carbo., 0 g fiber, 2 g pro.

Hot and Sassy Chicken Wings

Perfect for a spirited afternoon gathering, these succulent, crispy wings deliver a flavor kick.

Prep: 25 minutes **Bake:** 40 minutes
Marinate: 2 hours **Oven:** 375°F
Makes: 8 to 10 appetizer servings

10	chicken wings (about 2 pounds)
1	cup white wine vinegar
¼	cup packed brown sugar
¼	cup honey
2	teaspoons garlic powder
2	to 3 teaspoons bottled hot pepper sauce

Hot and Sassy Chicken Wings

1 teaspoon salt
1 teaspoon dried thyme, crushed
½ to 1 teaspoon cayenne pepper
Nonstick cooking spray

1. Cut off and discard tips from wings. Cut wings in half at joints to form 20 pieces. Place wing pieces in a large resealable plastic bag; set aside.

2. For marinade, in a small bowl whisk together vinegar, brown sugar, honey, garlic powder, hot pepper sauce, salt, thyme, and cayenne pepper. Pour over wings in bag; seal bag. Marinate in the refrigerator for 2 to 4 hours, turning bag occasionally.

3. Preheat oven to 375°F. Line a 15×10×1-inch baking pan with foil. Lightly coat a large roasting rack with nonstick cooking spray; set rack in prepared pan. Drain chicken wings, reserving marinade. Place wings on roasting rack; set aside.

4. Transfer marinade to a medium saucepan. Bring to boiling over medium-high heat. Boil gently, uncovered, about 10 minutes or until marinade is reduced to about ½ cup and is thick and slightly syrupy, stirring occasionally.

5. Brush wings on both sides with some of the reduced marinade. Bake for 30 minutes. Turn wings over; brush with remaining marinade. Bake about 10 minutes more or until chicken is no longer pink.

Per serving: 205 cal., 10 g total fat (3 g sat. fat), 47 mg chol., 331 mg sodium, 16 g carbo., 0 g fiber, 11 g pro.

morning favorites

During the holidays, daybreaks become extra special. Mornings offer a special time to treat houseguests and friends. From pancakes and waffles to make-ahead breakfast casseroles and simple bowl food, you will find lively and satisfying morning dishes on these pages.

Easy Huevos Rancheros Casserole,
page 55

Gingerbread Pancakes

If pancakes are standard fare on weekends at your house, swap them for a ginger-molasses version during the holidays. Any syrup will do, but you also could serve with lemon sauce or applesauce.

Start to Finish: 30 minutes **Makes:** 16 pancakes

2¼	cups all-purpose flour
1	tablespoon baking powder
2	teaspoons ground ginger
¼	teaspoon salt
2	eggs, lightly beaten
1¾	cups buttermilk
⅓	cup molasses
3	tablespoons cooking oil
	Desired syrup

1. In a large bowl combine flour, baking powder, ginger, and salt. In a medium bowl combine eggs, buttermilk, molasses, and oil. Add egg mixture all at once to flour mixture. Stir just until combined but still slightly lumpy.

2. Pour about ¼ cup batter onto a hot, lightly greased griddle or heavy skillet, spreading batter if necessary. Cook over medium-low heat for 2 to 3 minutes on each side or until pancakes have bubbly surfaces and edges are slightly dry. Serve warm with syrup.

Per pancake: 121 cal., 4 g total fat (1 g sat. fat), 28 mg chol., 121 mg sodium, 19 g carbo., 0 g fiber, 3 g pro.

Overnight Three-Grain Waffles

Cornmeal adds notable taste and texture to these light and fluffy waffles, while a rich and creamy pecan sauce makes this a breakfast worth remembering!

Prep: 25 minutes **Bake:** per waffle baker directions
Chill: up to 24 hours **Makes:** eight (4-inch) waffles

1¼	cups all-purpose flour
1	cup yellow cornmeal
½	cup oat bran
3	tablespoons sugar
1	package active dry yeast
½	teaspoon salt
2	cups milk
2	eggs
⅓	cup cooking oil
1	recipe Praline Sauce or maple syrup

1. In large mixing bowl combine flour, cornmeal, oat bran, sugar, yeast, and salt; add milk, eggs, and oil. Beat with an electric mixer on medium speed about 1 minute or until thoroughly combined. Cover batter loosely; chill for up to 24 hours.

2. Stir batter. Add batter to a preheated, lightly greased waffle baker according to manufacturer's directions. Close lid quickly; do not open until done. Bake according to manufacturer's directions. When done, use a fork to lift baked waffle off grid. Repeat with remaining batter. Serve warm with Praline Sauce.

Praline Sauce: In a small saucepan combine ¾ cup granulated sugar, ¾ cup packed brown sugar, and ½ cup half-and-half or light cream. Cook and stir over medium-high heat until boiling, stirring constantly to dissolve sugars. Boil, uncovered, for 1 minute. Remove from heat. Stir in ⅓ cup coarsely chopped pecans, 1 tablespoon butter or margarine, and ½ teaspoon vanilla. Makes 1½ cups.

Per waffle: 515 cal., 19 g total fat (5 g sat. fat), 67 mg chol., 212 mg sodium, 81 g carbo., 3 g fiber, 9 g pro.

Overnight Cranberry French Toast

If you could eat just one holiday dish, this rich, decadent, and beautiful indulgence would be it. Creamy yogurt and ricotta are spread between slices of whole wheat bread and joined by a tangy-nutty cranberry sauce.

Prep: 20 minutes **Bake:** 55 minutes
Chill: overnight **Oven:** 300°F/350°F
Makes: 6 servings

12	½-inch slices whole wheat bread, halved diagonally
6	eggs, lightly beaten
1	32-ounce carton vanilla low-fat yogurt
1	tablespoon finely shredded orange peel
½	cup orange juice

Overnight Three-Grain Waffles

¼   cup sugar
¼   teaspoon ground nutmeg
1   cup canned whole cranberry sauce
½   cup ricotta cheese
⅓   cup chopped pecans

1. Preheat oven to 300°F. Place bread on a large baking sheet. Bake, uncovered, for 10 minutes, turning once.

2. In a large bowl whisk together eggs, yogurt, orange peel, orange juice, sugar, and nutmeg until combined. Pour half of the egg mixture into a greased 3-quart rectangular baking dish.

3. Combine cranberry sauce and ricotta cheese. Spread evenly over half of the bread triangles; top with remaining triangles forming sandwiches. Arrange sandwiches on top of the egg mixture in baking dish. Slowly pour remaining egg mixture evenly over sandwiches, covering them. Cover and chill overnight.

4. Preheat oven to 350°F. Sprinkle pecans over sandwiches. Bake, uncovered, about 45 minutes or until set. If necessary to prevent overbrowning, cover with foil during the last 10 minutes of baking.

Per serving: 520 cal., 6 g total fat (5 g sat. fat), 230 mg chol., 466 mg sodium, 75 g carbo., 4 g fiber, 21 g pro.

Pumpkin Bread
French Toast

French Toast Casserole

*Many love this festive breakfast dish, both for its
infusion of orange liqueur and for the way it spends
the night in the refrigerator before baking. It is a
perfect choice for early morning meals.*

Prep: 20 minutes **Bake:** 40 minutes
Stand: 15 minutes **Chill:** up to 24 hours
Oven: 350°F **Makes:** 8 servings

1 **cup packed brown sugar**
½ **cup butter or margarine**
2 **tablespoons light-color corn syrup**

1 **1-pound loaf unsliced cinnamon bread,
   cut into 1 inch slices**
8 **eggs, lightly beaten**
3 **cups half-and-half or light cream**
2 **teaspoons vanilla**
½ **teaspoon salt**
1 **tablespoon orange liqueur (optional)**

1. In a medium saucepan combine brown sugar,
butter, and corn syrup. Cook and stir until mixture
comes to a boil. Boil, uncovered, for 1 minute.
Pour brown sugar mixture evenly into a 3-quart
rectangular baking dish.

2. Arrange bread slices on top of brown sugar mixture. Combine eggs, half-and-half, vanilla, and salt; pour evenly over bread slices. Cover and chill up to 24 hours.

3. Preheat oven to 350°F. Bake, uncovered, for 40 to 45 minutes or until top is puffy and brown and a knife inserted near center comes out clean. Let stand for 15 minutes before serving. If desired, drizzle with orange liqueur.

Per serving: 579 cal., 30 g total fat (16 g sat. fat), 279 mg chol., 692 mg sodium, 65 g carbo., 1 g fiber, 14 g pro.

Pumpkin Bread French Toast

Eggnog gives this French toast a distinctive holiday flavor. If you can't find pumpkin bread in your supermarket bakery, make your own or substitute cinnamon or banana bread.

Prep: 10 minutes **Cook:** 4 minutes per slice
Makes: 4 servings

- 4 eggs, lightly beaten
- 1 cup dairy eggnog or milk
- 1 teaspoon vanilla
- ½ teaspoon ground nutmeg
- 8 ½-inch slices pumpkin bread, cinnamon bread, or banana bread
   Maple syrup
   Butter or margarine (optional)
   Powdered sugar (optional)

1. In a shallow bowl beat together eggs, eggnog, vanilla, and nutmeg. Dip pumpkin bread slices quickly into egg mixture, coating both sides.

2. Heat a large nonstick skillet over medium heat; add half of the bread slices and cook for 2 to 3 minutes on each side or until golden brown. Repeat with remaining bread slices. Serve warm with maple syrup and, if desired, butter and powdered sugar.

Per serving: 643 cal., 26 g total fat (9 g sat. fat), 276 mg chol., 364 mg sodium, 93 g carbo., 2 g fiber, 12 g pro.

Easy Huevos Rancheros Casserole

Kicky Mexican-style eggs cook in a baking dish, perfect for serving at a buffet. The scent of cumin, garlic, and chili powder plus fresh cilantro lets you know what deliciousness lies ahead for your palate. See photo, page 51.

Prep: 15 minutes **Bake:** 35 minutes
Stand: 10 minutes **Oven:** 375°F
Makes: 12 servings

   Nonstick cooking spray
- 1 32-ounce package frozen fried potato nuggets
- 12 eggs
- 1 cup milk
- 1½ teaspoons dried oregano, crushed
- 1½ teaspoons ground cumin
- ½ teaspoon chili powder
- ¼ teaspoon garlic powder
- 1 8-ounce package shredded Mexican cheese blend
- 1 16-ounce jar thick and chunky salsa
- 1 8-ounce carton dairy sour cream
   Snipped fresh cilantro

1. Preheat oven to 375°F. Lightly coat a 3-quart rectangular baking dish with nonstick cooking spray. Arrange potato nuggets in dish.

2. In a large mixing bowl combine eggs, milk, oregano, cumin, chili powder, and garlic powder. Beat with a rotary beater or wire whisk until combined. Pour egg mixture over potato nuggets.

3. Bake for 35 to 40 minutes or until a knife inserted near center comes out clean. Sprinkle cheese evenly over egg mixture. Bake about 3 minutes more or until cheese melts. Let stand for 10 minutes before serving. Top with salsa, sour cream, and cilantro.

Per serving: 343 cal., 21 g total fat (9 g sat. fat), 238 mg chol., 823 mg sodium, 26 g carbo., 2 g fiber, 14 g pro.

Italian Breakfast Burrito Wraps

Artichoke hearts, basil pesto, mozzarella, and marinara are rolled in tortillas with prosciutto and baby spinach for a full-flavored Italian twist on a classic Mexican dish.

Start to Finish: 25 minutes **Makes:** 6 servings

2	tablespoons olive oil
2	cups fresh baby spinach, chopped
1	6-ounce jar marinated artichoke hearts, drained
3	ounces prosciutto, chopped
½	cup fresh basil, snipped
3	shallots, finely chopped
2	cloves garlic, minced
8	eggs
	Dash salt
	Dash ground black pepper
6	10-inch flour tortillas
½	cup purchased basil pesto
1½	cups shredded mozzarella cheese
1	15-ounce container refrigerated marinara sauce, heated

1. In a large skillet heat olive oil over medium heat. Add spinach, artichoke hearts, prosciutto, basil, shallots, and garlic. Cook and stir until spinach wilts.

2. In a medium bowl whisk together eggs, salt, and pepper. Pour over spinach mixture in skillet. Cook over medium heat, without stirring, until mixture begins to set on the bottom and around the edges. With a spatula, lift and fold the partially cooked egg mixture so the uncooked portion flows underneath. Continue cooking over medium heat for 2 to 3 minutes or until egg mixture is cooked through but is still glossy and moist. Remove skillet from heat.

3. Wrap tortillas in white paper towels. Microwave on 100 percent power (high) for 30 to 40 seconds or just until warm. Spread some of the pesto over each warm tortilla to within 1 inch of the edges; sprinkle with cheese. Divide egg mixture among tortillas; roll up. Serve with warm marinara sauce.

Per serving: 538 cal., 32 g total fat (9 g sat. fat), 317 mg chol., 1,371 mg sodium, 35 g carbo., 2 g fiber, 27 g pro.

Breakfast Vegetable-Pasta Frittata

Fritatta is generally cooked in a skillet to serve one or two. Here a cheesy fritatta is baked in a rectangular dish to make plenty for a house full of people.

Prep: 40 minutes **Bake:** 40 minutes **Oven:** 350°F
Makes: 12 servings

6	ounces dried spaghetti
2	tablespoons olive oil
¾	cup chopped onion
1½	cups sliced fresh mushrooms
1	medium zucchini, cut into thin bite-size strips (1½ cups)
1	medium red sweet pepper, cut into thin bite-size strips
2	cloves garlic, minced
1	teaspoon salt
1	teaspoon dried oregano, crushed
½	teaspoon ground black pepper
10	eggs
1¼	cups milk
½	cup grated Parmesan cheese
2	8-ounce packages cream cheese, cut into small cubes and softened
1½	cups shredded sharp cheddar cheese
1	recipe Sautéed Tomato Sauce

1. Cook spaghetti according to package directions; drain. Return spaghetti to saucepan; cover and keep warm.

2. Preheat oven to 350°F. In a large saucepan heat olive oil over medium heat; add onion. Cook and stir about 5 minutes or until tender. Add

Italian Breakfast
Burrito Wraps

mushrooms, zucchini, sweet pepper, and garlic. Cook and stir about 3 minutes more or just until vegetables are tender. Drain off liquid. Stir in salt, oregano, and black pepper; cool.

3. In a large mixing bowl beat eggs, milk, and Parmesan cheese with an electric mixer on low speed until combined. Add cream cheese; beat for 30 seconds.

4. Arrange spaghetti in the bottom of a greased 3-quart rectangular baking dish. Top with vegetable mixture. Sprinkle with cheddar cheese. Pour egg mixture evenly over cheese. Press down lightly with the back of a large spoon. Bake about 40 minutes or until frittata is set and light brown on the edges. Cut frittata into serving-size pieces. Serve with Sautéed Tomato Sauce.

Sautéed Tomato Sauce: In a medium saucepan heat 2 tablespoons butter or margarine over medium heat; add ¾ cup chopped onion. Cook and stir about 5 minutes or until onion is tender, stirring frequently. Add 2 cloves garlic, minced; cook and stir for 30 seconds. Carefully stir in one 28-ounce can Italian-style whole tomatoes in puree, undrained and cut up; half of a 6-ounce can (⅓ cup) tomato paste; ½ teaspoon sugar; ¼ teaspoon salt; and ¼ teaspoon ground black pepper. Bring to boiling; reduce heat. Simmer, uncovered, about 15 minutes or until desired consistency. If desired, stir in 1 teaspoon dried oregano, crushed. Cook for 5 minutes more. Makes about 4 cups.

Per serving: 407 cal., 28 g total fat (15 g sat. fat), 244 mg chol., 727 mg sodium, 22 g carbo., 2 g fiber, 18 g pro.

Southwestern Potato Breakfast Bake

Think quiche for a crowd, but with a hash-brown base and chiles and chili powder spiking the flavor. Serve with citrus juices and coffee, and your crowd is ready for the day.

Prep: 25 minutes **Bake:** 30 minutes
Stand: 10 minutes **Oven:** 375°F. **Makes:** 8 servings

    Nonstick cooking spray
½ of a 30-ounce package (5 cups) frozen
    shredded hash brown potatoes

Breakfast Vegetable-Pasta Frittata

¾ teaspoon seasoned salt
1 cup chopped onion
1 tablespoon olive oil
2 14½-ounce cans diced tomatoes and
   green chiles, undrained
1 teaspoon chili powder
¼ teaspoon ground black pepper
8 eggs
⅓ cup milk
1 cup shredded Mexican cheese blend

1. Preheat oven to 375°F. Lightly coat a 3-quart rectangular baking dish with nonstick cooking spray. Arrange potatoes in dish; sprinkle with ¼ teaspoon of the seasoned salt. Set aside.

2. In a large skillet cook onion in hot oil until tender. Add undrained tomatoes, chili powder, the remaining ½ teaspoon seasoned salt, and pepper. Bring to boiling; reduce heat. Simmer, uncovered, for 10 minutes, stirring occasionally. Spoon over potatoes in dish. In a large bowl whisk together eggs and milk; pour over tomato mixture in dish. Sprinkle with cheese.

3. Bake for 30 to 35 minutes or until set. Let stand 10 minutes before serving.

Per serving: 221 cal., 11 g total fat (5 g sat. fat), 225 mg chol., 635 mg sodium, 17 g carbo., 3 g fiber, 13 g pro.

Tex-Mex Breakfast Pizza

Prep: 25 minutes **Bake:** 8 minutes **Oven:** 375°F
Makes: 8 servings

> Nonstick cooking spray
1½ cups loose-pack frozen diced hash brown potatoes, thawed
¼ cup finely chopped green onions
1 to 2 canned jalapeño chile peppers, drained, seeded, and chopped*
½ teaspoon bottled minced garlic
¼ teaspoon ground cumin
1 cup refrigerated or frozen egg product, thawed
¼ cup milk
1 tablespoon snipped fresh cilantro
1 16-ounce Italian bread shell (Boboli)
½ cup shredded Monterey Jack cheese
1 small tomato, seeded and chopped

1. Preheat oven to 375°F. Lightly coat an unheated large skillet with nonstick cooking spray. Preheat skillet over medium heat. Add potatoes, green onions, chile peppers, garlic, and cumin. Cook and stir about 3 minutes or until vegetables are tender.

2. Combine egg product, milk, and cilantro. Add to potato mixture in skillet. Cook over medium heat, without stirring, until mixture begins to set on the bottom and around the edges. With a spatula, lift and fold the partially cooked egg mixture so the uncooked portion flows underneath. Continue cooking until egg mixture is cooked through but is still glossy and moist. Remove skillet from heat.

3. To assemble pizza, place the bread shell on a large baking sheet or 12-inch pizza pan; sprinkle with half of the cheese. Top with egg mixture, tomato, and the remaining cheese. Bake for 8 to 10 minutes or until cheese melts; cut into wedges.

***Note:** Because chile peppers contain oils that can burn skin and eyes, avoid direct contact with them as much as possible. When working with chile peppers, wear plastic or rubber gloves. If your bare hands do touch the peppers, wash them well with soap and warm water.

Per serving: 232 cal., 6 g total fat (2 g sat. fat), 9 mg chol., 465 mg sodium, 33 g carbo., 2 g fiber, 13 g pro.

Make-Ahead Brunch Lasagna Rolls

Lasagna noodles stand in for slices of bread, giving this make-head casserole a heartier texture. Swiss and Parmesan cheeses, Canadian-style bacon, spinach, and mustard combine to make a satisfying brunch dish.

Prep: 50 minutes **Bake:** 45 minutes
Chill: up to 24 hours **Oven:** 375°F
Makes: 6 servings

> Nonstick cooking spray
6 dried lasagna noodles
¼ cup butter or margarine
3 tablespoons all-purpose flour
1 tablespoon Dijon-style mustard
2 cups milk
6 ounces process Swiss or Gruyére cheese, torn or cut up
6 eggs
1 cup chopped Canadian-style bacon
1 10-ounce package frozen chopped spinach, thawed and well drained
¼ cup shredded Parmesan cheese

1. Lightly coat six 10- to 12-ounce au gratin dishes or individual casseroles with nonstick cooking spray; set aside. Cook lasagna noodles according to package directions; drain. Rinse with cold water; drain well and set aside.

2. Meanwhile, for sauce, in a large skillet melt 3 tablespoons of the butter over medium heat. Stir in flour, mustard, and ¼ teaspoon *ground black pepper*. Add 1¾ cups of the milk all at once. Cook and stir until thickened and bubbly. Reduce heat to low; stir in Swiss cheese until melted. Transfer sauce to a bowl.

3. In the same skillet melt the remaining 1 tablespoon butter. In a medium bowl beat together eggs, the remaining ¼ cup milk, and ¼ teaspoon *salt*; pour into skillet. Cook over medium heat, without stirring, until mixture begins to set on the bottom and around the edges. With a spatula, lift and fold partially cooked egg mixture so uncooked portion flows underneath. Continue cooking over medium heat for 2 to 3 minutes or until egg mixture is cooked through but still glossy and moist. Remove skillet from heat. Stir in ¼ cup of the sauce and the Canadian bacon.

Apple-Almond Cinnamon Strata

4. Stir ½ cup of the remaining sauce into the spinach. Divide spinach mixture evenly among the au gratin dishes. Spread about ½ cup of the egg mixture over the whole length of each lasagna noodle; roll up. Place one roll in each dish, seam side down. Spoon remaining sauce over rolls. Cover and chill for up to 24 hours.

5. Preheat oven to 375°F. Place dishes on a large baking sheet. Bake, covered, for 40 minutes. Uncover and sprinkle with Parmesan cheese. Bake, uncovered, about 5 minutes more or until heated through.

Per serving: 436 cal., 25 g total fat (12 g sat. fat), 276 mg chol., 1,123 mg sodium, 25 g carbo., 2 g fiber, 26 g pro.

Apple-Almond Cinnamon Strata

While most egg casseroles are savory, this one is sweet. Think apple pie, nutty custard.

Prep: 20 minutes **Bake:** 50 minutes
Stand: 15 minutes **Chill:** 2 hours **Oven:** 325°F
Makes: 8 servings

- 1 **1-pound loaf cinnamon-raisin bread, cut into 1-inch pieces**
- 8 **eggs, lightly beaten**
- 2 **cups milk**
- ¼ **teaspoon salt**
- ¼ **teaspoon almond extract**
- 1 **21-ounce can apple pie filling**
- ½ **cup slivered almonds, toasted (see Note, page 17)**
   Ground cinnamon or powdered sugar

1. Spread bread pieces in a greased 3-quart rectangular baking dish; set aside. In a large bowl whisk together eggs, milk, salt, and almond extract. Stir in apple pie filling and half of the almonds. Carefully pour apple mixture over the bread in baking dish. Press bread pieces down into the egg mixture with a wooden spoon. Sprinkle with remaining almonds. Cover and chill 2 to 24 hours.

2. Preheat oven to 325°F. Bake, uncovered, about 50 minutes or until the internal temperature registers 170°F on an instant-read thermometer. Let stand for 15 minutes before serving. Lightly sprinkle cinnamon or sift powdered sugar over the top before serving.

Per serving: 387 cal., 13 g total fat (3 g sat. fat), 216 mg chol., 422 mg sodium, 55 g carbo., 4 g fiber, 15 g pro.

Individual Ham and Cheese Quiches

1. Preheat oven to 400°F. Let refrigerated piecrusts stand at room temperature according to package directions. Cut each piecrust into four equal sections (eight sections total). Press one piecrust section into the bottom and up the sides of each of eight 4-inch fluted tart pans with removable bottoms. Trim the excess dough at top of pans.

2. Line each unpricked pastry shell with a double thickness of foil. Place tart pans on a baking sheet. Bake for 7 minutes. Remove foil. Bake for 2 to 3 minutes more or until pastry is set and dry. Remove from oven. Reduce oven temperature to 325°F.

3. In a medium bowl combine shredded cheese, sweet pepper, ham, green onion, flour, Italian seasoning, salt, and black pepper. Divide ham mixture evenly among the hot baked pastry shells.

4. In the same bowl beat together eggs and half-and-half. Pour egg mixture over ham mixture in each pastry shell. Bake about 20 minutes or until set. Let stand for 5 minutes before serving. If desired, garnish each quiche with fresh herb sprigs.

Per quiche: 317 cal., 20 g total fat (8 g sat. fat), 97 mg chol., 391 mg sodium, 28 g carbo., g fiber, 6 g pro.

Individual Ham and Cheese Quiches

Set an elegant breakfast table with solo quiches at each plate, or arrange all of them on a tiered cake pedestal.

Prep: 40 minutes **Bake:** 20 minutes
Stand: 5 minutes **Oven:** 400°F/325°F
Makes: 8 quiches

1	15-ounce package rolled refrigerated unbaked piecrusts (2 crusts)
½	cup shredded Italian cheese blend
½	cup finely chopped red sweet pepper
¼	cup finely chopped peppered or smoked cooked ham
1	tablespoon thinly sliced green onion or 1½ teaspoons snipped fresh chives
1½	teaspoons all-purpose flour
¼	teaspoon dried Italian seasoning, crushed
⅛	teaspoon salt
⅛	teaspoon ground black pepper
3	eggs, lightly beaten
½	cup half-and-half, light cream, or milk Fresh herb sprigs (such as basil, oregano, or thyme) (optional)

Sweet Breakfast Couscous

Instead of a bowl of steaming hot oatmeal, how about couscous? You'll love it for its quick prep as much as its sweet, nutty flavor.

Start to Finish: 10 minutes **Makes:** 4 servings

¾	cup quick-cooking couscous
¼	cup raisins
1	tablespoon packed brown sugar
¼	teaspoon ground cinnamon
1	cup milk
1	tablespoon maple syrup or honey Milk (optional)

1. In a 1- to 1½-quart microwave casserole combine couscous, raisins, brown sugar, and cinnamon. Stir in the 1 cup milk. Microwave, covered, on 100 percent power (high) for 3 to 4 minutes or until milk is absorbed, stirring once.

Let stand, covered, 3 minutes. Drizzle each serving with maple syrup. If desired, pass additional milk.

Per serving: 344 cal., 2 g total fat (1 g sat. fat), 5 mg chol., 34 mg sodium, 70 g carbo., 4g fiber, 11 g pro.

Tropical Ambrosia Salad

Choose this fruit mixture for its fresh, sunny flavors. Typically made with mandarin oranges and bananas, this salad uses exotic mango, papaya, and a rum-spiked sour cream dressing.

Start to Finish: 20 minutes **Makes:** 8 to 10 servings

- 1 **24-ounce jar refrigerated mango slices, drained and coarsely chopped**
- 1 **24-ounce jar refrigerated grapefruit sections, drained**
- 1 **20-ounce can pineapple chunks (juice pack), drained**
- 1 **recipe Sour Cream-Orange Dressing**
- ½ **cup large flaked coconut or dried coconut chips, toasted***
- 1 **to 2 tablespoons pomegranate seeds**

1. In a large bowl stir together mango, grapefruit, and pineapple. Add dressing, stirring gently to coat. Sprinkle with coconut and pomegranate seeds. Serve immediately.

Sour Cream-Orange Dressing: In a small bowl stir together ½ cup dairy sour cream; 2 tablespoons frozen orange juice concentrate, thawed; and 1 tablespoon packed brown sugar.

*Note: To toast coconut, spread in a single layer in a shallow baking pan. Bake in a 350°F oven 5 to 10 minutes or until golden brown, stirring once or twice. Watch carefully so coconut does not burn.

Per serving: 206 cal., 5 g total fat (4 g sat. fat), 5 mg chol., 48 mg sodium, 41 g carbo., 1 g fiber, 2 g pro.

Tropical Ambrosia Salad

surprising breads

Who can resist the goodness that awaits on the holiday breadboard? Moist challah, flaky biscuits, soft muffins, silky rolls, nutty bread, decadent coffee cake, light-as-air popovers—they are all here, tweaked and embellished to deliver an extra wave of deliciousness.

Quick Almond Stollen,
page 74

Orange and Chocolate Challah

Soft and sweet challah, traditional Jewish yeast bread, is a welcome base for shredded orange peel and orange liqueur.

Prep: 45 minutes **Rise:** 2 hours **Bake:** 35 minutes
Rest: 10 minutes **Oven:** 325°F
Makes: 16 servings

2¾ to 3¼ cups all-purpose flour
  1 package active dry yeast
  ¾ cup milk
  ½ cup sugar
  ¼ cup butter
  ½ teaspoon salt
  1 egg
  ½ cup chopped pecans
  ¼ cup chopped pitted dates
  1 tablespoon finely shredded orange peel
  1 tablespoon orange liqueur
  2 tablespoons unsweetened cocoa powder
     Milk
  1 recipe Two Glazes

1. In a large mixing bowl stir together 1½ cups of the flour and the yeast. In a medium saucepan heat and stir the ¾ cup milk, sugar, butter, and salt just until warm (120°F to 130°F) and butter almost melts; add to flour mixture along with egg. Beat with an electric mixer on low speed for 30 seconds, scraping sides of bowl constantly. Beat on high speed for 3 minutes. Using a wooden spoon, stir in ½ cup additional flour, pecans, and dates. Place one-third of the dough in a small bowl; set aside.

2. Stir orange peel and orange liqueur into the remaining dough. Stir in as much of the remaining flour as you can. Turn orange dough out onto a lightly floured surface. Knead in enough of the remaining flour to make a moderately soft dough that is smooth and elastic (3 to 5 minutes).

3. Shape dough into a ball. Place dough in a greased bowl; turn once to grease surface of dough. Cover and let rise in a warm place until double (about 1 to 1½ hours).

4. Stir cocoa powder and as much of the remaining flour as you can into the remaining one-third portion of dough. Repeat kneading and rising steps as for the orange dough.

5. Punch each dough down. Turn each dough out onto a lightly floured surface. Divide orange dough in half. Cover; let rest for 10 minutes. Meanwhile, lightly grease a large baking sheet. Shape each portion of dough into a 16-inch-long rope (3 ropes total). Line up ropes about 1 inch apart on prepared baking sheet with the chocolate rope in the center.

6. Starting in the middle of the ropes, loosely braid by bringing the left rope under the center rope. Next bring right rope under the new center rope. Repeat to the end. On the other end, braid by bringing alternate ropes over center rope from center to end. Press ends together to seal; tuck under. Cover; let rise in a warm place until nearly double (about 1 hour).

7. Preheat oven to 325°F. Brush loaf with additional milk. Bake about 35 minutes or until bread sounds hollow when lightly tapped. If necessary to prevent overbrowning, cover loosely with foil during the last 10 to 15 minutes of baking. Immediately remove from baking sheet. Cool on a wire rack. Drizzle with Two Glazes.

Two Glazes: In a medium bowl stir together 1½ cups powdered sugar and 4 teaspoons softened butter. Add enough warm water (1 to 2 tablespoons) to make icing drizzling consistency. Divide icing in half. Stir 1 teaspoon unsweetened cocoa powder into one half; add more warm water, a drop at a time, if necessary, until icing is drizzling consistency. Stir 1 teaspoon finely shredded orange peel and 1 teaspoon frozen orange juice concentrate, thawed, into the other half; add more warm water, a drop at a time, if necessary, until icing is drizzling consistency.

Per serving: 231 cal., 7 g total fat (3 g sat. fat), 24 mg chol., 111 mg sodium, 38 g carbo., 1 g fiber, 4 g pro.

Chocolate-Nut Brioche Loaves

Prep: 1¼ hours **Rise:** 3½ hours
Bake: 35 minutes **Chill:** overnight **Oven:** 350°F
Makes: 2 loaves (24 slices)

  2 packages active dry yeast
  ⅓ cup warm water (105°F to 115°F)
1½ cups butter, softened

Orange and
Chocolate Challah

¼ cup granulated sugar
3¾ cups all-purpose flour
⅓ cup milk
4 eggs
½ cup packed brown sugar
1 teaspoon ground cinnamon
⅔ cup miniature semisweet chocolate pieces
½ cup chopped pecans or almonds
1 tablespoon water
 Coarse sugar (optional)

1. In a small bowl dissolve yeast in warm water. Let stand 5 to 10 minutes to soften. In a very large mixing bowl beat butter, granulated sugar, and 1 teaspoon *salt* with an electric mixer on medium speed until fluffy. Beat in 1½ cups of the flour and the milk. Beat in 3 of the eggs. Add softened yeast mixture; beat well. Stir in the remaining flour. Transfer dough to a greased bowl (dough will be sticky). Cover; let rise in a warm place for 2 hours. Stir dough down; cover and chill overnight.

2. Grease two 8×4×2-inch loaf pans; set aside. In a small bowl combine brown sugar, cinnamon, chocolate pieces, and nuts; set aside.

3. Turn dough out onto a lightly floured surface; divide dough in half. Roll each dough half into a 14×8-inch rectangle; sprinkle each rectangle with some of the brown sugar mixture. Roll up each rectangle, starting from a short side. Pinch dough to seal seams. Place dough in prepared pans. Cover and let rise in a warm place for 1½ hours.

4. Preheat oven to 350°F. Combine remaining egg and water; lightly brush over tops of loaves. If desired, sprinkle tops with coarse sugar. Bake about 35 minutes or until golden brown and bread sounds hollow when lightly tapped. Immediately remove bread from pans. Cool on wire racks.

Per slice: 265 cal., 16 g total fat (9 g sat. fat), 66 mg chol., 194 mg sodium, 27 g carbo., 1 g fiber, 4 g pro.

Chocolately Butter-Nut
Cinnamon Rolls

Chocolatey Butter-Nut Cinnamon Rolls

It's the holidays, so why not have dessert for breakfast? Mixed nuts and chocolate chips make these cinnamon rolls unforgettable. Serve with mugs of coffee and glasses of cold milk.

Prep: 30 minutes **Rise:** 30 minutes
Bake: 30 minutes **Cool:** 5 minutes **Oven:** 375°F
Makes: 12 rolls

2	cups powdered sugar
⅔	cup whipping cream
1	cup chopped mixed nuts
½	cup packed brown sugar
1	tablespoon all-purpose flour
1	tablespoon ground cinnamon
2	16-ounce loaves frozen sweet roll or white bread dough, thawed
¼	cup butter, melted
½	cup semisweet chocolate pieces
½	cup chopped mixed nuts
¾	cup semisweet chocolate pieces
1½	teaspoons shortening

1. For topping, in a medium bowl stir together powdered sugar and whipping cream until smooth.

Divide mixture between two 2-quart rectangular or square baking dishes. Sprinkle the 1 cup chopped nuts evenly over mixture in baking dishes; set aside.

2. For filling, in a small bowl stir together brown sugar, flour, and cinnamon; set aside.

3. On a lightly floured surface, roll each loaf of dough into a 12×8-inch rectangle (if dough is difficult to roll out, let it rest a few minutes and try again). Brush dough rectangles with melted butter. Sprinkle filling, the ½ cup chocolate pieces, and the ½ cup chopped nuts evenly over each rectangle. Roll up each rectangle, starting from a long side. Pinch dough to seal seams. Slice each rolled rectangle into 6 equal pieces. Arrange 6 pieces, cut sides down, in each prepared dish. Cover and let rise in a warm place until nearly double in size (30 to 45 minutes). Use a greased toothpick to break any surface bubbles.

4. Preheat oven to 375°F. Bake for 30 to 35 minutes or until sides of rolls are brown and center rolls do not appear doughy (do not underbake*). If necessary to prevent overbrowning, cover loosely with foil during the last 15 to 20 minutes of baking. Cool in dishes on wire racks for 5 minutes; remove from dishes.

5. In a small saucepan combine the ¾ cup chocolate pieces and the shortening. Cook and stir over low heat until chocolate is melted and smooth; drizzle over cinnamon rolls. Serve warm.

*Note: The topping will turn to a caramel color as the rolls bake. If you pick up a baking dish, the topping underneath the rolls should appear caramel colored when the rolls are done.

Per roll: 605 cal., 29 g total fat (13 g sat. fat), 72 mg chol., 177 mg sodium, 82 g carbo., 4 g fiber, 10 g pro.

Cornmeal-Chive Batter Rolls

This reworked bread recipe makes a wonderful, savory roll.

Prep: 30 minutes **Rise:** 20 minutes
Bake: 18 minutes **Rest:** 10 minutes
Oven: 350°F **Makes:** 12 rolls

  1 tablespoon yellow cornmeal
  2 cups all-purpose flour
  1 package fast-rising active dry yeast
  ¼ teaspoon ground black pepper
  1 cup milk
  2 tablespoons sugar
  3 tablespoons butter
  ½ teaspoon salt
  1 egg
  ½ cup snipped fresh chives or ¼ cup
      finely chopped green onions
  ⅓ cup yellow cornmeal

1. Grease twelve 2½-inch muffin cups; sprinkle bottoms of cups with the 1 tablespoon cornmeal. Set aside. In a large mixing bowl combine 1¼ cups of the flour, yeast, and pepper; set aside.

2. In a small saucepan heat and stir milk, sugar, butter, and salt over medium heat just until warm (120°F to 130°F) and butter almost melts; add to flour mixture along with egg. Beat with an electric mixer on low to medium speed for 30 seconds, scraping bowl. Beat on high speed for 3 minutes. Stir in chives and the ⅓ cup cornmeal. Stir in the remaining ¾ cup flour (batter will be soft and sticky). Cover; let rest in a warm place 10 minutes. Spoon batter into prepared muffin cups. Cover and let rise in a warm place for 20 minutes.

3. Preheat oven to 350°F. Bake about 18 minutes or until golden brown. Cool in muffin cups on a wire rack for 5 minutes. Remove from muffin cups; serve warm.

Per roll: 140 cal., 4 g total fat (2 g sat. fat), 28 mg chol., 144 mg sodium, 21 g carbo., 1 g fiber, 4 g pro.

Cheddar-Corn Bread Rolls

Fill your bread basket with soft, crunchy rolls that blend cornmeal and cheddar bits into a hearty roll.

Prep: 10 minutes **Rise:** 20 minutes
Bake: 20 minutes **Rest:** 5 minutes
Oven: 375°F **Makes:** 15 rolls

  1 16-ounce package hot roll mix
  1 cup shredded cheddar, Monterey Jack,
      or Monterey Jack with jalapeño peppers
      cheese
  ⅓ cup cornmeal
  1¼ cups hot water (120°F to 130°F)
  2 tablespoons olive oil
  1 egg, lightly beaten
      Milk
      Cornmeal

1. In a large bowl stir together the flour and yeast packet from the hot roll mix; stir in cheese and the ⅓ cup cornmeal. Add the hot water, oil, and egg, stirring until combined.

2. Turn dough out onto a well-floured surface. Knead dough about 5 minutes or until smooth and elastic. Cover and let rest for 5 minutes. Lightly grease a 13×9×2-inch baking pan; set aside.

3. Divide dough into 15 pieces. Gently pull each dough piece into a ball, tucking edges under to make a smooth top. Arrange dough balls in prepared pan. Cover and let rise in a warm place for 20 minutes.

4. Preheat oven to 375°F. Brush dough balls with milk; sprinkle with additional cornmeal. Bake for 20 to 22 minutes or until golden. Remove rolls from pan. Cool on a wire rack.

Per roll: 180 cal., 5 g total fat (2 g sat. fat), 22 mg chol., 230 mg sodium, 27 g carbo., 0 g fiber, 7 g pro.

Parmesan Mini Dinner Rolls

Scented with basil, these soft dinner rolls are flecked with shreds of peppery Parmesan cheese.

Prep: 45 minutes **Rise:** 1½ hours **Bake:** 12 minutes
Rest: 10 minutes **Oven:** 400°F
Makes: 24 rolls

2½ to 2¾ cups all-purpose flour
 1 package active dry yeast
 ¼ cup finely shredded Parmesan cheese
 2 tablespoons snipped fresh basil
 2 tablespoons sugar
 1 cup warm water (120°F to 130°F)
 1 tablespoon milk
 2 tablespoons finely shredded Parmesan
    cheese

1. In a large bowl combine 1 cup of the flour, yeast, the ¼ cup Parmesan cheese, basil, sugar, and 1 teaspoon *salt*; add water. Beat with an electric mixer on low to medium speed for 30 seconds, scraping bowl. Beat on high speed 3 minutes. Stir in as much of the remaining flour as you can.

2. Turn dough out onto a lightly floured surface. Knead in enough of the remaining flour to make a moderately stiff dough that is smooth and elastic (6 to 8 minutes total). Shape dough into a ball. Place in a greased bowl; turn once to grease surface of dough. Cover; let rise in a warm place until double in size (about 1 hour).

3. Punch dough down. Turn dough out onto a lightly floured surface. Divide dough in half. Cover; let rest for 10 minutes. Lightly grease twenty-four 1¾-inch muffin cups; set aside.

4. Divide each dough half into 12 pieces. Gently pull each piece of dough into a ball, tucking edges under to make a smooth top. Place dough balls, smooth sides up, in prepared muffin cups. Cover and let rise in a warm place until nearly double in size (about 30 minutes).

5. Preheat oven to 400°F. Brush dough balls with milk; sprinkle with the 2 tablespoons Parmesan cheese. Bake for 12 to 15 minutes or until golden. Immediately remove rolls from pans; serve warm.

Per roll: 58 cal., 0 g total fat (0 g sat. fat), 1 mg chol., 119 mg sodium, 11 g carbo., 0 g fiber, 2 g pro.

Rosemary Satin Butterhorn Rolls

Prepare these silky-textured rolls for an elegant classic with a surprising new twist. Rosemary and onion infuse them with robust flavor.

Prep: 40 minutes **Rise:** 1½ hours **Bake:** 12 minutes
Rest: 10 minutes **Oven:** 400°F
Makes: 16 rolls

2½ to 3 cups all-purpose flour
 1 package active dry yeast
 ⅔ cup cream-style cottage cheese
 ¼ cup water
 ¼ cup butter
 2 tablespoons finely chopped onion
 ½ teaspoon dried rosemary, crushed
 1 egg
 ¼ cup butter, melted
 1 egg yolk
 1 tablespoon water

1. In a large mixing bowl stir together ¾ cup of the flour and the yeast. In a small saucepan heat and stir cottage cheese, the ¼ cup water, ¼ cup butter, onion, rosemary, and ½ teaspon *salt* just until warm (120°F to 130°F) and butter almost melts; add to flour mixture along with whole egg. Beat with an electric mixer on low speed for 30 seconds. Beat on high speed for 3 minutes. Using a wooden spoon, stir in as much of the remaining flour as you can.

2. Turn dough out onto a lightly floured surface. Knead in enough of the remaining flour to make a moderately stiff dough that is smooth and elastic (6 to 8 minutes total). Shape dough into a ball. Place in a greased bowl; turn once to grease surface of dough. Cover; let rise in a warm place until double in size (about 1 hour).

3. Punch dough down. Turn dough out onto a lightly floured surface. Divide dough in half. Cover; let rest for 10 minutes. Lightly grease baking sheets; set aside.

4. On a lightly floured surface, roll each dough half into a 10-inch circle; brush with the ¼ cup melted butter. Cut each dough circle into 8 wedges. To shape rolls, begin at wide end of each wedge and loosely roll toward the point. Place, point sides down, 2 to 3 inches apart on prepared baking sheets.

5. In a small bowl stir together egg yolk and the 1 tablespoon water; brush over rolls. Cover; let rise in a warm place until nearly double in size (about 30 minutes).

6. Preheat oven to 400°F. Bake for 12 to 15 minutes or until golden. Immediately remove rolls from baking sheets. Cool on wire racks.

Per roll: 141 cal., 7 g total fat (4 g sat. fat), 43 mg chol., 155 mg sodium, 160 g carbo., 1 g fiber, 4 g pro.

Eggnog Quick Bread

Some think that a sip of eggnog goes down too quickly. Relish that flavor in a quick bread this holiday season.

Prep: 25 minutes **Bake:** 50 minutes **Oven:** 350°F
Makes: 1 loaf (16 slices)

2¼ cups all-purpose flour
  2 teaspoons baking powder
  ½ teaspoon salt
  ¼ teaspoon freshly grated nutmeg or
     ground nutmeg
  2 eggs, lightly beaten
  1 cup sugar
  1 cup dairy or canned eggnog
  ½ cup butter, melted
  1 teaspoon vanilla
  ½ teaspoon rum extract (optional)
  1 cup slivered almonds, toasted
     (see Note, page 17)
  1 recipe Eggnog Icing

1. Preheat oven to 350°F. Grease the bottom and ½ inch up the sides of a 9×5×3-inch loaf pan or two 7½×3½×2-inch loaf pans; set aside. In a large bowl combine flour, baking powder, salt, and nutmeg. Make a well in center of flour mixture.

2. In a medium bowl stir together eggs, sugar, eggnog, butter, vanilla, and, if desired, rum extract. Add egg mixture all at once to flour mixture. Stir just until moistened (batter should be lumpy). Fold in the almonds.

3. Spoon batter into prepared pan(s). Bake for 50 to 55 minutes for 9×5×3-inch pan or 40 to 45 minutes for 7½×3½×2-inch pans or until a toothpick inserted in center comes out clean.

Rosemary Satin
Butterhorn Rolls

4. Cool in pan(s) on wire rack(s) for 10 minutes. Remove from pan(s). Cool completely on wire rack(s). Wrap and store overnight before slicing. Drizzle with Eggnog Icing. Let stand until set.

Eggnog Icing: In a small bowl combine ½ cup powdered sugar, ¼ teaspoon vanilla, and a dash freshly grated nutmeg or ground nutmeg. Stir in enough dairy or canned eggnog (2 to 3 teaspoons) until drizzling consistency.

Per slice: 244 cal., 11 g total fat (5 g sat. fat), 51 mg chol., 162 mg sodium, 33 g carbo., 1 g fiber, 5 g pro.

Orange-Date Pumpkin Bread

This holiday classic undergoes a healthy makeover with whole wheat flour, honey, and chewy dates. Tasty and filling, this bread is perfect for breakfast or snacking.

Prep: 30 minutes **Bake:** 50 minutes **Oven:** 350°F
Makes: 2 loaves (32 slices)

    2   cups all-purpose flour
    1⅓ cups whole wheat flour
    2   teaspoons baking powder
    1   teaspoon ground nutmeg
    ½   teaspoon salt
    ½   teaspoon baking soda
    1   15-ounce can pumpkin
    ¾   cup sugar
    4   eggs, lightly beaten
    ½   cup honey
    ⅓   cup cooking oil
    1   teaspoon finely shredded orange peel
    ⅓   cup orange juice
    ½   cup chopped walnuts or pecans
    ½   cup snipped pitted dates or raisins

1. Preheat oven to 350°F. Grease the bottom and ½ inch up the sides of two 8×4×2-inch loaf pans; set aside. In a large bowl stir together all-purpose flour, whole wheat flour, baking powder, nutmeg, salt, and baking soda.

2. In a medium bowl stir together pumpkin, sugar, eggs, honey, oil, orange peel, and orange juice. Stir pumpkin mixture into flour mixture just until combined. Fold in nuts and dates. Spoon batter in prepared pans.

3. Bake about 50 minutes or until a toothpick inserted near centers comes out clean. Cool in pans on wire racks for 10 minutes. Remove from pans. Cool completely on wire racks. Wrap and store overnight before slicing.

Per slice: 126 cal., 4 g total fat (1 g sat. fat), 0 mg chol., 87 mg sodium, 22 g carbo., 2 g fiber, 3 g pro.

Apple Pie Bread

Apple Pie Bread

Move over, apple pie! This bread, with its moist apple flavor and crunchy streusel-nut topping, may become the new American standard.

Prep: 35 minutes **Bake:** 1 hour **Oven:** 350°F
Makes: 1 loaf (14 slices)

    ½   cup butter, softened
    1   cup sugar
    ¼   cup buttermilk
    2   teaspoons baking powder
    2   eggs
    1   teaspoon vanilla
    2   cups all-purpose flour
    ½   teaspoon salt
    2   cups shredded, peeled apples
        (about 4 medium)
    1   cup chopped walnuts or pecans
    ½   cup raisins
    1   recipe Streusel-Nut Topping

1. Preheat oven to 350°F. Grease the bottom and ½ inch up the sides of a 9×5×3-inch loaf pan; set aside.

2. In a large mixing bowl beat butter with an electric mixer on medium to high speed for 30 seconds. Beat in sugar until combined.

Overnight
Coffee Cake

Add buttermilk and baking powder; beat until combined. Add eggs and vanilla; beat until combined. Add flour and salt; beat until combined. Stir in apples, nuts, and raisins.

3. Spoon batter into prepared pan. Sprinkle Streusel-Nut Topping over batter. Bake for 60 to 65 minutes or until a wooden toothpick inserted near the center comes out clean. Cool in pan on a wire rack for 10 minutes. Remove from pan. Cool completely on wire rack. Wrap and store overnight before slicing.

Streusel-Nut Topping: In a small bowl combine ¼ cup packed brown sugar and 3 tablespoons all-purpose flour. Using a pastry blender, cut in 2 tablespoons butter until mixture resembles coarse crumbs. Stir in ⅓ cup chopped walnuts or pecans.

Per slice: 332 cal., 17 g total fat (6 g sat. fat), 52 mg chol., 193 mg sodium, 43 g carbo., 2 g fiber, 5 g pro.

Overnight Coffee Cake

If you love the aroma and freshness of just-out-of-the-oven baked goods but balk at the notion of early morning prep, this treat is for you.

Prep: 25 minutes Bake: 35 minutes
Chill: up to 24 hours Oven: 350°F
Makes: 15 servings

3	cups all-purpose flour
1½	teaspoons baking powder
1½	teaspoons baking soda
1	teaspoon salt
1	cup butter, softened
1¼	cups granulated sugar
3	eggs
1	15-ounce carton ricotta cheese
¾	cup chopped nuts
½	cup packed dark brown sugar
2	tablespoons toasted wheat germ
1	tablespoon ground cinnamon
1	teaspoon ground nutmeg

1. Lightly grease the bottom and ½ inch up the sides of a 13×9×2-inch baking pan; set aside. In a large bowl combine flour, baking powder, baking soda, and salt; set aside.

2. In a large mixing bowl beat butter on medium speed for 30 seconds. Add granulated sugar; beat until combined. Add eggs one at a time, beating well after each addition. Beat in ricotta cheese. Beat in as much of the flour mixture as you can. Stir in any remaining flour mixture. Spread batter in prepared pan. In another bowl combine nuts, brown sugar, wheat germ, cinnamon, and nutmeg. Sprinkle evenly over batter. Cover and chill for up to 24 hours.

3. Preheat oven to 350°F. Uncover and bake for 35 to 40 minutes or until a wooden toothpick inserted near the center comes out clean. Cool slightly; serve warm.

Per serving: 397 cal., 22 g total fat (10 g sat. fat), 91 mg chol., 438 mg sodium, 43 g carbo., 1 g fiber, 8 g pro.

Orange-Cranberry
Muffins

Orange-Cranberry Muffins

Using a packaged biscuit mix really speeds up the preparation of these delicious breakfast muffins. Adding a little dry pudding mix keeps them moist.

Prep: 20 minutes **Bake:** 15 minutes **Oven:** 400°F
Makes: 12 muffins

- 2 **cups packaged biscuit mix**
- ½ **cup sugar**
- 3 **tablespoons vanilla instant pudding and pie filling**
- 2 **teaspoons finely shredded orange peel**
- ½ **teaspoon ground cinnamon**
- 1 **egg, lightly beaten**
- ½ **cup milk**
- ¼ **cup orange juice**
- 2 **tablespoons cooking oil**
- ¾ **cup dried cranberries**

1. Preheat oven to 400°F. Grease twelve 2½-inch muffin cups; set aside. In a medium bowl stir together biscuit mix, sugar, pudding, orange peel, and cinnamon. Make a well in the center of the dry mixture.

2. In a small bowl combine egg, milk, orange juice, and oil. Add egg mixture all at once to dry mixture. Stir just until moistened (batter should be lumpy). Fold in cranberries.

3. Spoon batter into prepared muffin cups, filling each about two-thirds full. Bake about 15 minutes or until golden. Cool in muffin cups on a wire rack for 5 minutes. Remove muffins from cups; serve warm.

Per muffin: 183 cal., 6 g total fat (1 g sat. fat), 18 mg chol., 307 mg sodium, 32 g carbo., 1 g fiber, 2 g pro.

Pumpkin-Black Walnut Muffins

Prep: 30 minutes **Bake:** 20 minutes **Oven:** 400°F
Makes: 12 muffins

½	of an 8-ounce tub cream cheese
2	tablespoons packed brown sugar
1½	cups all-purpose flour
2	teaspoons baking powder
½	teaspoon baking soda
¼	to ½ teaspoon ground nutmeg
¼	teaspoon salt
1	egg, lightly beaten
⅔	cup canned pumpkin
½	cup buttermilk
⅓	cup packed brown sugar
⅓	cup butter, melted
1	recipe Streusel Topper

1. Preheat oven to 400°F. Grease twelve 2½-inch muffin cups; set aside. In a small bowl stir together cream cheese and the 2 tablespoons brown sugar until smooth; set aside.

2. In a large bowl stir together flour, baking powder, baking soda, nutmeg, and salt. Make a well in the center of the flour mixture. In a medium bowl combine egg, pumpkin, buttermilk, the ⅓ cup brown sugar, and melted butter. Add egg mixture all at once to flour mixture. Stir just until moistened (batter should be lumpy).

3. Place a rounded tablespoon of batter into each prepared muffin cup. Add about 2 teaspoons of the cream cheese mixture to each cup. Divide remaining batter among the cups, filling to the top. Sprinkle Streusel Topper over muffin batter in cups, pressing lightly into batter (cups will be very full).

4. Bake for 20 to 25 minutes or until a wooden toothpick inserted near centers comes out clean. Cool in muffin cups on a wire rack for 5 minutes. Remove from muffin cups; serve warm.

Streusel Topper: In a bowl combine ⅔ cup all-purpose flour and ⅓ cup packed brown sugar. Using a pastry blender, cut in ¼ cup butter until mixture resembles coarse crumbs. Stir in ½ cup coarsely chopped black walnuts or English walnuts.

Per muffin: 294 cal., 15 g total fat (7 g sat. fat), 52 mg chol., 272 mg sodium, 33 g carbo., 1 g fiber, 5 g pro.

Onion Muffins with Rosemary and Pine Nuts

These fragrant, savory muffins are a fitting complement to a glorious main dish and a change of pace from yeast rolls or biscuits.

Prep: 15 minutes **Bake:** 20 minutes **Oven:** 350°F
Makes: 12 muffins

1½	cups coarsely chopped sweet onions (such as Vidalia or Walla Walla)
⅔	cup butter
2	cups all-purpose flour
⅓	cup sugar
3	to 4 teaspoons finely snipped fresh rosemary or 1 teaspoon dried rosemary, finely crushed
2	teaspoons baking powder
½	teaspoon salt
2	eggs, lightly beaten
⅓	cup milk
¼	cup pine nuts or slivered almonds, toasted and coarsely chopped (see Note, page 17)

1. Preheat oven to 350°F. Grease twelve 2½-inch muffin cups or line with paper bake cups; set aside. In a large skillet cook onions in hot butter about 8 minutes or until tender; cool slightly.

2. In a large bowl combine flour, sugar, rosemary, baking powder, and salt. Make a well in the center of the flour mixture. In another bowl combine eggs and milk. Add egg mixture and onion mixture all at once to flour mixture. Stir just until moistened (batter should be lumpy). Gently stir in pine nuts.

3. Spoon batter into prepared muffin cups. Bake about 20 minutes or until tops are golden brown and a wooden toothpick inserted in centers comes out clean. Cool in muffin cups on a wire rack for 5 minutes. Remove from muffin cups; serve warm.

Per muffin: 232 cal., 13 g total fat (7 g sat. fat), 63 mg chol., 246 mg sodium, 24 g carbo., 1 g fiber, 4 g pro.

Gingerbread-Sour Cream Muffins

Worthy of being the starring attraction at a brunch or tea, this gingerbread goes fancy in a muffin cup.

Prep: 20 minutes **Bake:** 18 minutes **Oven:** 400°F
Makes: 12 muffins

2	cups all-purpose flour
1	tablespoon minced fresh ginger or 1 teaspoon ground ginger
2	teaspoons baking powder
¾	teaspoon ground allspice or ground cinnamon
¼	teaspoon baking soda
¼	teaspoon salt
¼	cup butter
⅓	cup milk
1	egg, lightly beaten
1	8-ounce carton dairy sour cream
¼	cup packed brown sugar
¼	cup mild-flavor molasses
2	tablespoons granulated sugar
2	tablespoons finely chopped crystallized ginger

1. Preheat oven to 400°F. Grease bottoms of twelve 2½-inch muffin cups; set aside.

2. In a medium bowl combine flour, fresh ginger, baking powder, allspice, baking soda, and salt. Using a pastry blender, cut in butter until mixture resembles coarse crumbs.

3. In another bowl stir together milk, egg, sour cream, brown sugar, and molasses. Add egg mixture all at once to flour mixture. Stir just until moistened (batter should be a little lumpy).

4. Spoon batter into prepared muffin cups, filling each nearly full. In a small bowl combine granulated sugar and crystallized ginger; sprinkle over muffin batter in cups. Bake for 18 to 20 minutes or until golden and a wooden toothpick inserted in centers comes out clean. Cool in muffin cups on a wire rack for 5 minutes. Remove from muffin cups; serve warm.

Per muffin: 211 cal., 9 g total fat (5 g sat. fat), 37 mg chol., 168 mg sodium, 30 g carbo., 1 g fiber, 4 g pro.

Quick Almond Stollen

This easy stollen recipe is perfect for the hectic holiday season. It is leavened with baking powder instead of yeast, so there is no waiting for yeast to rise. See photo, page 63.

Prep: 40 minutes **Bake:** 40 minutes **Oven:** 325°F
Makes: 2 loaves (24 servings)

2¼	cups all-purpose flour
½	cup sugar
1½	teaspoons baking powder
⅓	cup butter, cut up
¾	cup tropical blend mixed dried fruit bits*
½	cup slivered almonds
1	egg, lightly beaten
1	8-ounce carton dairy sour cream
1	teaspoon vanilla
½	cup almond paste
1	tablespoon finely chopped crystallized ginger
1	recipe Almond Icing

1. Preheat oven to 325°F. Line a large baking sheet with parchment paper; set aside. In a large bowl stir together the flour, sugar, baking powder, and ¼ teaspoon *salt*. Using a pastry blender, cut in butter until mixture resembles coarse crumbs. Stir the fruit bits and almonds into the flour mixture. Make a well in the center of the flour mixture.

2. In a medium bowl stir together the egg, sour cream, and vanilla. Add the sour cream mixture all at once to the flour mixture. Stir just until moistened. Turn dough out onto a lightly floured surface; gently knead dough until it holds together. Divide the dough in half. Using well-floured hands, pat each dough half into a 7×5-inch oval on the prepared baking sheet.

3. Crumble the almond paste into a small bowl; stir in ginger. Sprinkle half of the almond mixture over each oval. Fold over a long side of each oval to within 1 inch of the opposite long side; press edges to lightly seal.

4. Bake for 40 to 45 minutes or until light brown around the edges and a wooden toothpick inserted near the center comes out clean. Transfer to a wire rack. Drizzle Almond Icing over warm stollen. Cool completely. Wrap and store for up to 24 hours.

Sage and Pepper
Popovers

Almond Icing: In a small bowl stir together 1 cup powdered sugar and ⅛ teaspoon almond extract. Stir in enough milk (1 to 2 tablespoons) to make drizzling consistency.

*Note: If desired, soak dried fruit bits in 3 tablespoons rum for 1 hour; drain well.

Per serving: 170 cal., 7 g total fat (3 g sat. fat), 20 mg chol., 77 mg sodium, 25 g carbo., 1 g fiber, 3 g pro.

Sage and Pepper Popovers

Sage is a familiar holiday herb, but it is not common in light popovers. Chopped sage and freshly ground black pepper give the traditional popover a flavor punch.

Prep: 15 minutes **Bake:** 40 minutes **Oven:** 400°F
Makes: 6 popovers

- 1 **tablespoon shortening or nonstick cooking spray**
- 2 **eggs, lightly beaten**
- 1 **cup milk**
- 1 **tablespoon olive oil**
- 1 **cup all-purpose flour**
- 2 **tablespoons grated Parmesan cheese**

- 2 **teaspoons finely snipped fresh sage or thyme or ½ teaspoon dried sage or thyme, crushed**
- ½ **teaspoon salt**
- ½ **teaspoon freshly ground black pepper**

1. Preheat oven to 400°F. Using ½ teaspoon shortening for each cup, grease the bottoms and sides of six cups of a popover pan or six 6-ounce custard cups. (Or lightly coat cups with cooking spray.) If using custard cups, place cups in a 15×10×1-inch baking pan; set aside.

2. In a bowl use a rotary beater or wire whisk to beat eggs, milk, and oil until combined. Add flour; beat until smooth. Stir in Parmesan cheese, sage, salt, and pepper. Fill the prepared cups half full with batter. Bake about 40 minutes or until firm.

3. Immediately after removing from oven, prick each popover with a fork to let steam escape. Turn off oven. For crisper popovers, return to oven for 5 to 10 minutes or until desired crispness. Remove popovers from cups; serve warm.

Per popover: 167 cal., 8 g total fat (2 g sat. fat), 75 mg chol., 260 mg sodium, 18 g carbo., 1 g fiber, 6 g pro.

Sweet Potato
Biscuits

Sweet Potato Biscuits

Bright orange sweet potatoes bring color and nutrients to tempting light, flaky potato biscuits.

Prep: 25 minutes **Bake:** 15 minutes **Oven:** 400°F
Makes: 16 biscuits

1   egg, lightly beaten
1   cup cooked, mashed sweet potatoes*
     or mashed canned sweet potatoes
¼   cup sugar
1   cup milk
3   cups all-purpose flour
4   teaspoons baking powder
1   tablespoon snipped fresh sage
     or 1 teaspoon dried sage, crushed
1½ teaspoons salt
¾   teaspoon baking soda
½   cup shortening
1   egg white, lightly beaten (optional)
16 small fresh sage leaves (optional)

1. Preheat oven to 400°F. In a medium bowl combine egg, mashed sweet potatoes, and sugar. Beat with a fork until smooth; stir in milk. Set aside.

2. In a large bowl stir together flour, baking powder, sage, salt, and baking soda. Using a pastry blender, cut in shortening until mixture resembles coarse crumbs. Make a well in the center of flour mixture. Add sweet potato mixture; stir just until combined.

3. Turn dough out onto a well-floured surface. Knead dough for 10 to 12 strokes or until nearly smooth. Lightly roll or pat dough until ½ inch thick. Cut dough with a floured 2½-inch biscuit cutter, rerolling scraps as necessary and dipping cutter into flour between cuts.

4. Place dough circles 1 inch apart on an ungreased large baking sheet. If desired, brush dough circles with egg white; top with a fresh sage leaf. Bake about 15 minutes or until biscuits are golden. Remove from baking sheet; serve warm.

*Note: For 1 cup mashed sweet potatoes, peel 2 medium sweet potatoes (about 1 pound); cut into 1½-inch chunks. Cook, covered, in enough boiling water to cover for 25 to 30 minutes or until very tender; drain. Mash with a potato masher or beat with an electric mixer.

Per biscuit: 180 cal., 7 g total fat (2 g sat. fat), 14 mg chol., 354 mg sodium, 25 g carbo., 1 g fiber, 4 g pro.

Peppery White Cheddar Biscuits

Full-flavored white cheddar and cracked pepper give melt-in-your-mouth biscuits a lively flavor. They are excellent with ham, prime rib, or to use for little sandwiches.

Prep: 25 minutes **Bake:** 13 minutes **Oven:** 400°F
Makes: 18 biscuits

- 4   cups all-purpose flour
- 2   tablespoons baking powder
- ½   teaspoon salt
- ½   cup shortening
- ¼   cup butter
- 1½ cups shredded sharp white cheddar cheese
- 2   to 3 teaspoons coarsely ground black pepper
- 1½ cups milk
- 1   egg, lightly beaten
- 1   teaspoon water

1. Preheat oven to 400°F. Lightly grease a large baking sheet; set aside. In a large bowl combine flour, baking powder, and salt. Using a pastry blender, cut in shortening and butter until mixture resembles coarse crumbs. Stir in cheese and

pepper. Make a well in the center of the flour mixture. Add milk all at once. Stir just until moistened.

2. Turn dough out onto a lightly floured surface. Knead dough 10 to 12 strokes or until nearly smooth. Divide dough in half. Lightly roll or pat each half into a 6-inch square that is about 1 inch thick. Using a sharp knife, cut each dough square into 2-inch squares. Combine egg and water; brush over tops of biscuits.

3. Place dough squares on prepared baking sheet. Bake for 13 to 15 minutes or until golden. Remove from baking sheet; serve warm.

Per biscuit: 247 cal., 14 g total fat (6 g sat. fat), 34 mg chol., 314 mg sodium, 24 g carbo., 1 g fiber, 7 g pro.

Peppery White Cheddar Biscuits

after-dinner sweets

These are the pièces de résistance that crown a particularly celebratory meal. We recommend a pause before this final course, perhaps a stroll around the neighborhood, before coming back to enjoy a fabulous finish, whether the confection be a masterful pie, pudding, or cake; a delicate tiramisu or cream puff; or a richer-than-Trump cheesecake.

Black Forest Cake Ball,
page 90

Extreme Chocolate Pie

Most chocolate lovers agree that if one chocolate is good, two are better. With that in mind, we added an ultra-rich brownie crust to a much-loved French silk chocolate pie.

Prep: 35 minutes **Bake:** 20 minutes **Chill:** 4 hours
Oven: 350°F **Makes:** 10 servings

- 1   8-ounce package brownie mix
- 1   cup sugar
- ¾   cup butter
- 6   ounces unsweetened chocolate, melted and cooled
- 1   teaspoon vanilla
- ¾   cup refrigerated or frozen egg product, thawed
- 1   recipe Sweetened Whipped Cream (page 82)
- 1   1.45-ounce bar dark sweet chocolate, shaved or coarsely chopped

1. Preheat oven to 350°F. Grease a 9-inch pie plate; set aside. Prepare brownie mix according to package directions; spread in the bottom of the prepared pie plate. Bake for 20 to 25 minutes or until a toothpick inserted in center comes out clean. Cool on a wire rack.

2. For filling, in a medium mixing bowl beat sugar and butter with an electric mixer on medium speed about 4 minutes or until fluffy. Stir in the melted chocolate and vanilla. Gradually add egg product, beating on low speed until combined. Beat on medium to high speed about 1 minute or until light and fluffy, scraping sides of bowl frequently.

3. Spread filling over baked brownie layer. Cover and chill for 4 to 24 hours. Just before serving, top with Sweetened Whipped Cream; sprinkle with shaved chocolate.

Per serving: 468 cal., 32 g total fat (19 g sat. fat), 74 mg chol., 246 mg sodium, 48 g carbo., 3 g fiber, 6 g pro.

Decadent Chocolate-Mixed Nut Tart

Why should pecans have all the sweet, buttery pie fun? Mixed nuts and semisweet chocolate pieces take pecan pie from awesome to sophisticated.

Prep: 30 minutes **Bake:** 1 hour **Oven:** 350°F
Makes: 10 to 12 servings

- 1   recipe Butter Pastry
- 4   eggs
- 1¼ cups light-color corn syrup
- ¾   cup sugar
- ¼   cup unsalted butter, melted
- 1   teaspoon vanilla
- 1¼ cups salted mixed nuts
- 1   cup miniature semisweet chocolate pieces
- 1   tablespoon shortening
- 1   recipe Sweetened Whipped Cream (page 82) (optional)

1. Preheat oven to 350°F. On a lightly floured surface, roll chilled Butter Pastry from center to edges into a 13-inch circle. Wrap pastry around a rolling pin. Unroll into a 9×2-inch fluted tart pan that has a removable bottom. Press pastry into fluted sides; trim edges. Do not prick pastry.

2. For filling, in a bowl beat eggs with a whisk. Whisk in corn syrup, sugar, butter, vanilla, and dash *salt*. Stir in nuts and ½ cup of the chocolate pieces. Place tart pan in a foil-lined shallow baking pan. Pour filling into pastry-lined tart pan.

3. To prevent overbrowning, cover edges with foil. Bake for 25 minutes. Remove foil. Bake for 35 to 40 minutes more or until center seems set when gently shaken. Cool on a wire rack. Cover and chill within 2 hours.

Decadent Chocolate-Mixed Nut Tart

4. In a small saucepan combine the remaining ½ cup chocolate pieces and shortening. Cook and stir over low heat until melted and smooth. Cool slightly.

5. Remove side of tart pan. Transfer melted chocolate to a resealable plastic bag. Cut a small hole in one corner of the bag and drizzle melted chocolate over each serving. If desired, top with Sweetened Whipped Cream.

Butter Pastry: In a medium bowl stir together 1½ cups all-purpose flour, 2 tablespoons sugar, ½ teaspoon baking powder, and ⅛ teaspoon salt. Using a pastry blender, cut in ¼ cup cold unsalted butter until pieces are pea-size. In a small bowl beat together 1 egg and 1 tablespoon ice water with a fork. Gradually stir egg mixture into flour mixture. Using your fingers, gently knead the mixture just until it forms a ball. (If dough won't form a ball, add another 1 tablespoon ice water, a little at a time.) Don't overknead; the dough should feel slightly sticky. Use your hands to slightly flatten dough into a disk about 6 inches in diameter. Wrap the disk in plastic wrap; chill for 45 to 60 minutes or until dough is firm and easy to handle.

Per serving: 546 cal., 28 g total fat (12 g sat. fat), 131 mg chol., 227 mg sodium, 68 g carbo., 4 g fiber, 9 g pro.

Chocolate Chess Pie

Lemon chess pie lovers will find their beloved thick, creamy chess texture featured in a cocoa-based chocolate pie.

Prep: 25 minutes **Bake:** 1 hour **Oven:** 350°F
Makes: 8 to 10 servings

1	recipe Pastry for Single-Crust Pie
2	cups sugar
¼	cup unsweetened cocoa powder
1	tablespoon cornmeal
1	tablespoon all-purpose flour
½	teaspoon salt
4	eggs, lightly beaten
½	cup milk
½	cup butter, melted
1	teaspoon vanilla
1	cup chopped pecans
	Whipped cream (optional)

Chocolate Chess Pie

1. Preheat oven to 350°F. Prepare and roll out Pastry for a Single-Crust Pie; set aside.

2. For filling, in a large bowl combine sugar, cocoa powder, cornmeal, flour, and salt. In a medium bowl whisk together eggs, milk, butter, and vanilla. Stir egg mixture into sugar mixture until smooth. Stir in pecans.

3. Pour filling into pastry-lined pie plate. Bake about 1 hour or until filling is set and crust is golden. If crust begins to brown too fast, reduce oven temperature to 325°F and cover edge of crust with foil. Cool on a wire rack. (Filling will fall slightly during cooling.) Cover and chill within 2 hours; chill for up to 24 hours. If desired, top with whipped cream.

Pastry for Single-Crust Pie: In a medium bowl stir together 1¼ cups all-purpose flour and ¼ teaspoon salt. Using a pastry blender, cut in ⅓ cup shortening until pieces are pea-size. Sprinkle 1 tablespoon cold water over part of the flour mixture; gently toss with a fork. Push moistened dough to the side of the bowl. Sprinkle additional cold water, 1 tablespoon at a time, over flour mixture until all of the dough is moistened (use 4 to 5 tablespoons water total). Form dough into a ball. On a lightly floured surface, slightly flatten dough. Roll dough from center to edges into a 12-inch circle. Wrap pastry around a rolling pin. Unroll into a 9-inch pie plate. Ease pastry into pie plate, being careful not to stretch it. Trim pastry to ½ inch beyond edge of pie plate. Fold under extra pastry. Crimp edge as desired. Do not prick pastry.

Per serving: 598 cal., 33 g total fat (11 g sat. fat), 138 mg chol., 342 mg sodium, 71 g carbo., 2 g fiber, 8 g pro.

Pumpkin-Pecan Pie

*If you can't decide between pumpkin or pecan pie,
try this mouthwatering combo of the two.*

Prep: 25 minutes **Bake:** 50 minutes **Oven:** 350°F
Makes: 8 servings

- 1 recipe Pastry for Single-Crust Pie (page 81)
- 3 eggs, lightly beaten
- 1 15-ounce can pumpkin
- ½ cup sugar
- ½ cup dark-color corn syrup
- 1 teaspoon vanilla
- ¾ teaspoon ground cinnamon
- 1 cup chopped pecans

1. Preheat oven to 350°F. Prepare and roll out
Pastry for Single-Crust Pie; set aside.

2. For filling, in medium bowl combine eggs,
pumpkin, sugar, corn syrup, vanilla, and cinnamon.
Carefully pour filling into pastry-lined pie plate.
Sprinkle with pecans.

3. Bake for 50 to 55 minutes or until a knife
inserted near center comes out clean. Cool on wire
rack. Cover and chill within 2 hours.

Per serving: 391 cal., 20 g total fat (4 g sat. fat), 79 mg chol.,
133 mg sodium, 50 g carbo., 3 g fiber, 6 g pro.

Pumpkin-Apple Butter Pie

*Fine chefs say that if an ingredient dominates, it is
too much. Subtlety is the goal, and apple butter is the
answer in this version of a classic holiday treat.*

Prep: 30 minutes **Bake:** 55 minutes **Oven:** 375°F
Makes: 8 to 10 servings

- 1 recipe Pastry for Single-Crust Pie (page 81)
- 1 15-ounce can pumpkin
- ½ cup packed brown sugar
- ½ cup apple butter
- 1 teaspoon ground cinnamon
- ½ teaspoon ground ginger
- ¼ teaspoon salt
- ⅛ teaspoon ground cloves
- 2 eggs, lightly beaten
- 1 egg yolk, lightly beaten
- ½ cup whipping cream

- ½ cup chopped pecans or walnuts
- 2 tablespoons butter, softened
- 2 tablespoons all-purpose flour
- 2 tablespoons packed brown sugar
- 1 recipe Sweetened Whipped Cream
   (optional)

1. Preheat oven to 375°F. Prepare and roll out
Pastry for Single-Crust Pie; set aside.

2. For filling, in a medium bowl combine pumpkin,
the ½ cup brown sugar, the apple butter, cinnamon,
ginger, salt, and cloves. Add eggs and egg yolk;
beat with a fork just until combined. Gradually
add whipping cream, stirring until combined.

3. Carefully pour filling into pastry-lined pie plate.
To prevent overbrowning, cover edge of pie with
foil. Bake for 20 minutes. Remove foil. Bake for
20 minutes more. Meanwhile, in a small bowl
combine nuts, butter, flour, and the 2 tablespoons
brown sugar; sprinkle over the pie.

4. Bake for 15 to 20 minutes more or until a knife
inserted near the center comes out clean. Cool
on a wire rack. Cover and chill within 2 hours.
If desired, top with Sweetened Whipped Cream.

Sweetened Whipped Cream: In a large chilled
mixing bowl combine 1 cup whipping cream,
2 tablespoons sugar, and ½ teaspoon vanilla. Beat
with chilled beaters of an electric mixer on medium
speed until soft peaks form (tips curl over).

Per serving: 478 cal., 24 g total fat (8 g sat. fat), 107 mg chol.,
206 mg sodium, 62 g carbo., 4 g fiber, 6 g pro.

Country-Style Pear and Mincemeat Tart

*Pears and cranberries join mincemeat in a rustic-style
crust for a luscious treat that is over-the-top when
served with ice cream.*

Prep: 20 minutes **Bake:** 20 minutes **Oven:** 425°F
Makes: 8 servings

- ½ of a 15-ounce package rolled refrigerated
   unbaked piecrusts (1 crust)
- 3 tablespoons granulated sugar
- 1 teaspoon ground cinnamon

Country-Style Pear
and Mincemeat Tart

2   medium pears, peeled, cored, and
     cut into ½-inch slices
½   cup chopped pecans
⅓   cup dried cranberries
⅔   cup canned mincemeat
     Milk
     Coarse sugar
     Vanilla ice cream (optional)

1. Preheat oven to 425°F. Let refrigerated piecrust stand at room temperature according to package directions. Line a large baking sheet with parchment paper; set aside. In a large bowl combine granulated sugar and cinnamon. Add pear slices, pecans, and cranberries; toss to coat.

2. Place piecrust on prepared baking sheet. Spread mincemeat over crust to within 2 inches of edges. Mound pear mixture over mincemeat. Fold edges of pastry 2 inches up and over pear mixture, pleating edges as necessary. Brush folded edges lightly with milk; sprinkle with coarse sugar.

3. Bake 20 to 25 minutes or until crust is golden and pears are just tender. Serve warm. If desired, serve with vanilla ice cream.

Per serving: 279 cal., 12 g total fat (3 g sat. fat), 3 mg chol., 180 mg sodium, 42 g carbo., 2 g fiber, 2 g pro.

Cheesy Apple Pie

moistened dough to side of bowl. Sprinkle
additional cold water, 1 tablespoon at a time, over
flour mixture until all of the dough is moistened.
Form dough into a ball.

2. On a lightly floured surface, slightly flatten
dough. Roll dough from center to edges into a
12-inch circle. Wrap pastry around a rolling pin.
Unroll into a 9-inch pie plate. Ease pastry into pie
plate, being careful not to stretch it. Trim pastry to
½ inch beyond edge of pie plate. Fold under extra
pastry. Crimp edge as desired. Do not prick pastry.

3. For filling, in a large bowl combine apples, sugar,
the 2 tablespoons flour, cinnamon, and remaining
¼ teaspoon salt. Transfer filling to pastry-lined pie
plate. Sprinkle with remaining ½ cup cheese.
Sprinkle Crunch Topper evenly over filling.

4. To prevent overbrowning, cover edge of pie with
foil. Bake for 40 minutes. Remove foil. Bake about
20 minutes more or until fruit is tender and top is
golden brown. Cool on a wire rack.

Crunch Topper: In a bowl combine ¾ cup
all-purpose flour, ⅔ cup sugar, and ¼ teaspoon salt.
Using a pastry blender, cut in ⅓ cup butter until
mixture is crumbly.

Per serving: 497 cal., 21 g total fat (10 g sat. fat), 35 mg chol.,
288 mg sodium, 72 g carbo., 2 g fiber, 7 g pro.

Cheesy Apple Pie

*A slice of sharp cheddar served alongside apple pie is
heavenly tasting. For a twist, blend cheddar cheese
into the pastry and crunchy crumb topping.*

Prep: 45 minutes **Bake:** 1 hour **Oven:** 375°F
Makes: 8 servings

1¼	cups all-purpose flour
½	teaspoon salt
⅓	cup butter-flavor shortening
1	cup finely shredded cheddar cheese
4	to 5 tablespoons cold water
6	cups thinly sliced, peeled cooking apples (such as Granny Smith or Rome Beauty) (about 2¼ pounds)
¾	cup sugar
2	tablespoons all-purpose flour
1	teaspoon ground cinnamon
1	recipe Crunch Topper

1. Preheat oven to 375°F. In a medium bowl stir
together the 1¼ cups flour and ¼ teaspoon of the
salt. Using a pastry blender, cut in shortening until
pieces are pea-size. Stir in ½ cup of the cheese.
Sprinkle 1 tablespoon of the cold water over part
of the flour mixture; gently toss with a fork. Push

Apple-Cranberry-Hazelnut Pie

*Does your family love apple pie? See if their taste
buds are awakened by presenting this snappy twist.
Ruby-red cranberries join tart apples in the filling,
and rich hazelnuts in the pastry and crumb topping
add elegance and a fresh dimension.*

Prep: 1¼ hours **Bake:** 1½ hours **Oven:** 375°F
Makes: 12 servings

1	recipe Hazelnut Pastry
1	cup sugar
½	cup all-purpose flour
2	teaspoons finely shredded orange peel
¼	teaspoon salt
9	cups thinly sliced, peeled cooking apples (such as Rome Beauty or Granny Smith) (about 3 pounds)

2 cups fresh cranberries
3 tablespoons butter
1 recipe Hazelnut-Pine Nut Streusel
   Cinnamon or vanilla ice cream (optional)

1. Preheat oven to 375°F. On a lightly floured surface, slightly flatten Hazelnut Pastry. Roll dough from center to edges into a 12-inch circle. Pastry will be tender. Wrap pastry around a rolling pin. Unroll into a 9-inch springform pan. Fit pastry into the pan and up the sides. Press together any tears with your fingers; pat into place. Trim pastry even with top edge of pan. Do not prick pastry.

2. For filling, in a very large bowl combine sugar, flour, orange peel, and salt. Add apples and cranberries. Toss to coat. Mound mixture into the pastry-lined springform pan (pan will be full). Dot with butter. Sprinkle Hazelnut-Pine Nut Streusel over the filling.

3. Place springform pan in a shallow baking pan. To prevent overbrowning, cover with foil. Bake for 1¼ hours. Remove foil. Bake for 15 to 30 minutes more or until fruit is tender and filling is bubbly. Cool in springform pan on a wire rack. Run a thin spatula or knife around the edge of the crust. Remove side of springform pan; cut into wedges. If desired, serve with ice cream.

Hazelnut Pastry: In a medium bowl stir together 1⅓ cups all-purpose flour, ⅓ cup ground hazelnuts (filberts), 1 tablespoon packed brown sugar, and ¼ teaspoon salt. Using a pastry blender, cut in ½ cup butter-flavor shortening until pieces are pea-size. Sprinkle 1 tablespoon cold water over part of the flour mixture; gently toss with a fork. Push moistened dough to side of bowl. Sprinkle additional cold water, 1 tablespoon at a time, over flour mixture until all of the dough is moistened (use 3 to 4 tablespoons cold water total). Form dough into a ball.

Hazelnut-Pine Nut Streusel: In a small bowl stir together ½ cup all-purpose flour and ⅓ cup packed brown sugar. Using a pastry blender, cut in 3 tablespoons butter until mixture resembles coarse crumbs. Stir in ½ cup coarsely chopped hazelnuts (filberts) and ¼ cup pine nuts.

Per serving: 432 cal., 22 g total fat (6 g sat. fat), 15 mg chol., 142 mg sodium, 58 g carbo., 4 g fiber, 5 g pro.

Red Velvet Cupcakes with Peppermint Frosting

For quick peppermint frosting, stir together two 16-ounce cans cream cheese frosting and ½ teaspoon peppermint extract.

Prep: 20 minutes **Bake:** 18 minutes **Oven:** 350°F
Makes: 30 to 32 cupcakes

1 package 2-layer-size German chocolate cake mix
1 8-ounce carton dairy sour cream
¾ cup water
⅓ cup cooking oil
3 eggs
1 1-ounce bottle (2 tablespoons) red food coloring
1 recipe Peppermint Frosting
   Small peppermint candies (optional)

1. Preheat oven to 350°F. Line thirty to thirty-two 2½-inch muffins cups with paper bake cups; set aside.

2. In a large mixing bowl beat cake mix, sour cream, water, oil, eggs, and food coloring with an electric mixer on low speed for 30 seconds. Scrape sides of bowl. Beat on medium speed for 2 minutes more. Fill each muffin cup half full of batter.

3. Bake for 18 to 20 minutes or until a toothpick inserted near centers comes out clean. Cool cupcakes in pans on wire racks for 5 minutes. Remove cupcakes from pans; cool completely on wire racks. Frost cupcakes generously with Peppermint Frosting. Cover and chill in an airtight container for up to 2 days. If desired, just before serving top cupcakes with peppermint candies.

Peppermint Frosting: In a large mixing bowl beat one 8-ounce package softened cream cheese, ¼ cup softened butter, and ½ teaspoon peppermint extract with an electric mixer on medium speed until light and fluffy. Gradually beat in one 1-pound package powdered sugar (about 4 cups) and 1 to 3 tablespoons milk until spreading consistency.

Per cupcake: 212 cal., 10 g total fat (4 g sat. fat), 37 mg chol., 173 mg sodium, 30 g carbo., 0 g fiber, 2 g pro.

Brown Sugar-Pear Pound Cake

Moister than refined white sugar, brown sugar adds flavor depth to traditional pound cake. A splash of brandy makes this version even more festive.

Prep: 45 minutes **Bake:** 70 minutes
Cool: 10 minutes **Oven:** 350°F **Makes:** 16 servings

1½	cups butter
5	eggs
3½	cups all-purpose flour
1½	teaspoons baking powder
½	teaspoon salt
3	cups packed brown sugar
1	tablespoon vanilla
¾	cup milk
¼	cup pear brandy, pear liqueur, brandy, or orange juice
2¼	cups firm, ripe pears, peeled, cored, and cut into ¼-inch pieces
2	to 3 teaspoons finely shredded orange peel
⅓	cup granulated sugar
⅓	cup pear brandy, pear liqueur, brandy, or orange juice
1	recipe Sweetened Whipped Cream (page 82) (optional)

1. Allow butter and eggs to stand at room temperature for 30 minutes. Generously grease and flour a 10-inch fluted tube pan; set aside.

2. Preheat oven to 350°F. In a large bowl stir together flour, baking powder, and salt; set aside. In a very large mixing bowl beat butter with an electric mixer on medium to high speed for 30 seconds. Add brown sugar and vanilla; beat on high speed about 3 minutes or until mixture is smooth and light. Add eggs one at a time, beating after each addition just until combined.

3. Alternately add milk, the ¼ cup pear brandy, and flour mixture to egg mixture, beating after each addition just until combined. Fold in pears and orange peel. Spread batter evenly in prepared pan.

4. Bake for 70 to 80 minutes or until golden brown and a long wooden skewer inserted near the center comes out clean. Cool cake in pan on a wire rack for 10 minutes.

5. Meanwhile, for glaze, in a small saucepan combine granulated sugar and the ⅓ cup pear

Brown Sugar-Pear Pound Cake

brandy. Cook and stir over medium heat just until mixture boils and sugar dissolves.

6. Remove cake from pan; place on a wire rack. Place waxed paper under the wire rack. Use a pastry brush to brush warm glaze over entire cake surface. Cool completely. If desired, serve with Sweetened Whipped Cream.

Per serving: 491 cal., 19 g total fat (12 g sat. fat), 113 mg chol., 257 mg sodium, 70 g carbo., 1 g fiber, 5 g pro.

Lime-Infused Coconut Pound Cake

This pound cake takes on a tropical twist, thanks to lime and coconut.

Prep: 30 minutes **Bake:** 65 minutes
Oven: 325°F **Makes:** 16 servings

	Nonstick spray for baking
1	cup butter, softened
½	cup shortening
2½	cups granulated sugar
5	eggs
3	cups all-purpose flour
1	teaspoon baking powder
½	cup cream of coconut
¼	cup lime juice
1	teaspoon vanilla
1	cup flaked coconut, toasted (see Note, page 61)
1	cup powdered sugar
1	tablespoon milk
½	teaspoon finely shredded lime peel
¼	teaspoon coconut extract
	Toasted coconut shards* (optional)

1. Preheat oven to 325°F. Lightly coat a 10-inch fluted tube pan with nonstick spray for baking; set pan aside. In a very large mixing bowl beat butter and shortening with an electric mixer on medium speed until combined. Gradually add granulated sugar, beating about 10 minutes or until light and fluffy. Add eggs one at a time, beating for 1 minute after each addition and scraping bowl frequently.

2. Stir together flour and baking powder. In a small bowl combine cream of coconut, lime juice, vanilla, and ¼ cup *water*. Alternately add flour mixture and cream of coconut mixture to egg mixture, beating after each addition just until combined. Fold in coconut. Spread batter evenly in prepared pan.

3. Bake for 65 to 75 minutes or until a long wooden skewer inserted near center comes out clean. Cool cake in pan on a wire rack for 10 minutes. Remove cake from pan. Cool thoroughly on wire rack.

4. For icing, in a small bowl combine powdered sugar, milk, lime peel, and coconut extract. Stir in enough additional milk, 1 teaspoon at a time, to make icing drizzling consistency. Drizzle over cooled cake. If desired, sprinkle with coconut shards.

***Note:** To make toasted coconut shards, preheat oven to 350°F. With a vegetable peeler, shave curls of fresh coconut. Spread in a single layer in a shallow baking pan. Bake for 5 to 10 minutes or until light brown.

Per serving: 479 cal., 25 g total fat (14 g sat. fat), 97 mg chol., 148 mg sodium, 61 g carbo., 1 g fiber, 5 g pro.

Lime-Infused Coconut Pound Cake

Gingered Carrot Cake

Prep: 40 minutes **Bake:** 30 minutes **Cool:** 1 hour
Oven: 350°F **Makes:** 12 to 16 servings

2	cups all-purpose flour
2	cups sugar
2	teaspoons baking powder
½	teaspoon baking soda
3	cups finely shredded carrots
4	eggs, lightly beaten
¾	cup cooking oil
¾	cup mixed dried fruit bits
2	teaspoons grated fresh ginger or
	¾ teaspoon ground ginger
1	recipe Orange Cream Cheese Frosting

1. Preheat oven to 350°F. Grease and lightly flour two 9×1½-inch round baking pans*; set pans aside.

2. Combine flour, sugar, baking powder, and baking soda. Combine carrots, eggs, oil, dried fruit bits, and ginger. Stir egg mixture into flour mixture. Pour batter into prepared pans.

3. Bake for 30 to 35 minutes or until a wooden toothpick inserted in centers comes out clean. Cool in pans on wire racks for 10 minutes. Remove cake layers from pans. Cool thoroughly on wire racks. Frost tops and sides with Orange Cream Cheese Frosting. Cover and refrigerate for up to 3 days.

Orange Cream Cheese Frosting: In a bowl beat two 3-ounce packages softened cream cheese, ½ cup softened butter, and 1 tablespoon orange juice with an electric mixer on medium speed until fluffy. Gradually beat in 2 cups powdered sugar. Gradually beat in an additional 2½ to 2¾ cups powdered sugar until spreading consistency. Stir in ½ teaspoon finely shredded orange peel.

***Note:** The 9-inch round baking pans need to be at least 1½ inches deep or the batter could overflow during baking. If your round pans aren't deep enough, use one greased 13×9×2-inch baking pan. Prepare batter as directed above; spread in prepared pan. Bake in a 350°F oven about 40 minutes or until a toothpick inserted in center comes out clean. Cool completely in pan on wire rack.

Per serving: 677 cal., 28 g total fat (10 g sat. fat), 106 mg chol., 238 mg sodium, 104 g carbo., 1 g fiber, 6 g pro.

White Chocolate-Peppermint Dream Cake

cover recipe

Prep: 45 minutes **Bake:** 25 minutes
Oven: 350°F **Cool:** 1 hour **Chill:** up to 4 hours
Makes: 12 to 16 servings

3	eggs
1½	cups all-purpose flour
1½	teaspoons baking powder
1½	cups sugar
¾	cup milk
3	tablespoons butter
½	teaspoon peppermint extract
1½	teaspoons red food coloring
1	recipe Fluffy White Chocolate Frosting

1. Allow eggs to stand at room temperature for 30 minutes. Meanwhile, grease bottoms of two 8x1½-inch round baking pans. Line bottoms with waxed paper; grease and lightly flour pans; set aside.

2. Preheat oven to 350°F. In a small bowl stir together flour, baking powder, and ¼ teaspoon *salt*; set aside. In a medium mixing bowl beat eggs with an electric mixer on high speed about 4 minutes or until thick and lemon colored. Gradually add sugar, beating on medium speed for 4 to 5 minutes or until light and fluffy. Add flour mixture; beat on low to medium speed just until combined.

3. In a small saucepan heat and stir milk and butter just until butter melts. Add milk mixture and peppermint extract to batter, beating until combined. Divide batter in half. Spread half of the batter evenly in one of the prepared baking pans. Stir food coloring into the remaining batter; spread evenly in the other prepared baking pan. Bake for 25 to 30 minutes or until a wooden toothpick inserted near the centers comes out clean. Cool in pans on wire racks for 10 minutes. Remove cakes from pans. Peel off waxed paper. Cool completely on wire racks. Cut each cake layer in half horizontally to make a total of 4 layers.

4. To assemble, place 1 of the white cake layers on a serving plate; spread ¾ cup of the Fluffy White Chocolate Frosting evenly over the cake. Top with 1 of the red cake layers; spread another ¾ cup of the frosting evenly over the red cake. Top with the remaining white cake layer; spread another ¾ cup frosting evenly over cake. Top with remaining red cake layer. Spread frosting over top and sides of cake. If desired, sprinkle *white chocolate curls* and *coarsely chopped candy canes* over top of cake. Cover and chill for up to 4 hours. Store any leftover cake in the refrigerator.

Fluffy White Chocolate Frosting: In a medium saucepan heat and stir ½ cup whipping cream and 2 tablespoons butter over medium heat until butter melts. Remove saucepan from heat; add 8 ounces chopped high-quality white chocolate. Let stand, uncovered, for 5 minutes; whisk until smooth. Stir in ½ teaspoon peppermint extract.

In a large chilled mixing bowl beat 2 cups whipping cream with an electric mixer on medium speed until soft peaks form; fold in half of the white chocolate mixture at a time.

Per serving: 530 cal., 32 g total fat (20 g sat. fat), 139 mg chol., 195 mg sodium, 54 g carbo., 0 g fiber, 6 g pro.

Figgy Pudding Cake

Soft rich figs mingle in an espresso-drenched spice cake for a sophisticated dessert to serve with honey hard sauce. Baked in a fluted tube pan, this cake is a show stopper.

Prep: 45 minutes **Bake:** 45 minutes
Cool: 10 minutes **Oven:** 350°F **Makes:** 16 servings

1	pound dried figs, stems removed
1¾	cups water
1	package 2-layer-size spice cake mix
1	cup walnuts, toasted and chopped (see Note, page 17)
½	cup brewed espresso or strong coffee Powdered sugar
1	recipe Honey Hard Sauce

Figgy Pudding Cake

Festive Jam-and-Cannoli Cake Roll

1. Generously grease and flour a 10-inch fluted tube pan; set aside. In a medium saucepan combine figs and water. Bring to boiling. Remove saucepan from heat; let stand, covered, for 10 minutes. Transfer fig mixture to a food processor. Cover and process until figs are chopped.

2. Preheat oven to 350°F. Prepare cake mix according to package directions, except replace water with the fig mixture. Stir walnuts into batter. Pour batter into prepared pan.

3. Bake for 45 to 50 minutes or until a long wooden skewer inserted in the center comes out clean. Cool in pan on a wire rack for 10 minutes. Remove cake from pan. Place cake on a wire rack; place a shallow baking pan under the wire rack. Poke holes all over cake with a long-tined fork. Spoon espresso over cake. Cool completely. Wrap cake in plastic wrap and store at room temperature for up to 1 week.

4. Just before serving, sift powdered sugar over cake. Serve with Honey Hard Sauce. If desired, garnish with *fresh raspberries* and *fresh mint*.

Honey Hard Sauce: In a medium mixing bowl beat 1 cup softened butter and ¼ cup honey until smooth. Cover and chill until needed.

Per serving: 426 cal., 25 g total fat (9 g sat. fat), 72 mg chol., 303 mg sodium, 51 g carbo., 3 g fiber, 4 g pro.

Festive Jam-and-Cannoli Cake Roll

Prep: 30 minutes **Bake:** 12 minutes **Cool:** 1 hour
Chill: up to 2 hours **Oven:** 375°F **Makes:** 10 servings

½	cup all-purpose flour
1	teaspoon baking powder
¼	teaspoon salt
4	egg yolks
½	teaspoon vanilla
⅓	cup granulated sugar
2	tablespoons butter, melted
4	egg whites
¼	teaspoon cream of tartar
½	cup granulated sugar
¾	cup finely chopped pistachio nuts
	Powdered sugar
¾	cup strawberry jam
1	recipe Cannoli Filling
	Semisweet chocolate shavings (optional)

1. Preheat oven to 375°F. Grease and lightly flour a 15×10×1-inch baking pan; set aside. Stir together flour, baking powder, and salt; set aside.

2. In a medium mixing bowl beat egg yolks and vanilla with an electric mixer on high speed about 5 minutes or until thick and lemon colored. Gradually add the ⅓ cup granulated sugar, beating on medium speed until sugar is almost dissolved. Fold in melted butter. Thoroughly wash beaters.

3. In a large mixing bowl beat egg whites and cream of tartar on medium speed until soft peaks form (tips curl). Gradually add the ½ cup granulated sugar, beating on high speed until stiff peaks form (tips stand straight). Fold yolk mixture into beaten egg white mixture. Sprinkle flour mixture over egg mixture; fold in gently just until combined. Spread batter evenly in prepared pan. Sprinkle with nuts.

4. Bake for 12 to 15 minutes or until top springs back when lightly touched. Immediately loosen edges of cake; turn cake out onto a towel sprinkled with powdered sugar. Roll towel and cake into a spiral, starting from a short side of cake. Cool on a wire rack.

5. Unroll cake; remove towel. Spread jam evenly over cake to within 1 inch of edges. Carefully spread Cannoli Filling evenly on top of jam. Reroll cake. Cover and chill for up to 2 hours.

6. To serve, sprinkle top of cake with additional powdered sugar and chocolate shavings.

Cannoli Filling: Combine 1 cup ricotta cheese, 3 tablespoons sugar, and ½ teaspoon vanilla; stir in ⅓ cup finely chopped semisweet chocolate.

Per serving: 320 cal., 12 g total fat (4 g sat. fat), 99 mg chol., 187 mg sodium, 47 g carbo., 2 g fiber, 8 g pro.

Black Forest
Cake Ball

Black Forest Cake Ball

*This scrumptious chocolate-cherry cake bakes in a
mixing bowl for a "dome" presentation. Creamy
frosting embellishes this holiday dessert.*

Prep: 20 minutes **Bake:** 1¼ hours **Cool:** 4 hours
Oven: 325°F **Makes:** 16 servings

1	package 2-layer-size devil's food cake mix
1	21-ounce can cherry pie filling
⅓	cup cooking oil
2	eggs
4	ounces bittersweet or semisweet chocolate, chopped
1	recipe Creamy Frosting
2	ounces white baking chocolate, grated
1	recipe Chocolate-Dipped Maraschino Cherries

1. Preheat oven to 325°F. Grease and flour a
10-cup round oven-safe mixing bowl (bowl should
be 8 to 8½ inches across the top); set aside.

2. In a large mixing bowl beat together cake mix,
pie filling, oil, and eggs with an electric mixer on
medium to high speed until combined. Continue
beating for 1 minute more. Fold in bittersweet
chocolate. Pour batter into prepared bowl.

3. Bake for 1¼ to 1½ hours or until a long wooden
skewer inserted near the center comes out clean.
Cool in bowl on a wire rack for 10 minutes. Remove
from bowl. Cool at least 4 hours on a wire rack.

4. Transfer cake to a cake plate or platter. Spread
Creamy Frosting over top and sides of cake;
sprinkle with white chocolate. Cover and
refrigerate for up to 12 hours. Just before serving,
top with Chocolate-Dipped Maraschino Cherries.

Creamy Frosting: In a medium mixing bowl beat
⅔ cup purchased crème fraîche or dairy sour
cream, ⅔ cup whipping cream, and ½ cup
powdered sugar with an electric mixer on medium
speed until mixture forms soft peaks.

Chocolate-Dipped Maraschino Cherries:
Let 8 maraschino cherries with stems stand on paper
towels until drained thoroughly. Pat dry; set aside.
In a small microwave-safe dish microwave ½-ounce
chopped white baking chocolate on 100 percent power
(high) about 30 seconds or until melted, stirring once.
In another small microwave-safe dish microwave
1 tablespoon bittersweet chocolate baking pieces on
100 percent power (high) for 20 to 30 seconds or
until melted, stirring once. Dip cherries in melted
white chocolate. Place cherries, stem sides up,
on a waxed paper-lined baking sheet. Drizzle with
melted bittersweet chocolate. Let stand until set.

Per serving: 383 cal., 22 g total fat (9 g sat. fat), 55 mg chol.,
298 mg sodium, 46 g carbo., 2 g fiber, 4 g pro.

Easy Bûche de Nöel

*If your family tires from assembling gingerbread
houses, ask them to join you in making a super-
simple yule log cake. This version includes lots of
helping opportunities that shave preparation time.*

Prep: 45 minutes **Bake:** 15 minutes **Cool:** 2 hours
Chill: 4 hours **Makes:** 16 servings

1	14- to 16-ounce package angel food cake mix
⅓	cup unsweetened cocoa powder Powdered sugar
1	recipe Chocolate Cream
1	16-ounce can chocolate fudge frosting Chocolate curls (optional)

1. Preheat oven as directed on cake mix package. Grease two 15×10×1-inch baking pans. Line bottoms of pans with waxed paper or parchment paper; grease papers. Set aside.

2. In a large mixing bowl, stir together cake mix and cocoa powder. Prepare cake mix according to package directions. Divide batter evenly between prepared pans.* Using a table knife, gently cut through the batter to remove any air pockets.

3. Bake about 15 minutes or until cakes spring back when lightly touched. Immediately loosen edges of one cake from pan and turn cake out onto a towel sprinkled with powdered sugar. Remove waxed paper. Roll towel and cake into a spiral, starting from a short side. Repeat with the other cake and another powdered sugar-coated towel. Cool completely. Meanwhile, prepare Chocolate Cream.

4. Unroll cakes; remove towels. Spread cakes with Chocolate Cream to within 1 inch of the edges. Roll up cakes. Trim ends.

5. To assemble, using a long serrated knife, diagonally cut one cake roll into one-third and two-third pieces. Arrange the whole cake roll and two-thirds of the other cake roll on a platter with the diagonal cut on the end to form a log. Frost log with chocolate frosting. Arrange the other one-third of the cake roll to form a branch. Frost branch (do not frost ends). Using the tines of a fork or knife, score the cake lengthwise to resemble bark. Refrigerate 4 to 12 hours before serving. Garnish with chocolate curls, if desired. To serve, slice with a serrated knife, wiping knife and dipping in hot water between each cut.

Chocolate Cream: In a large chilled mixing bowl beat 2 cups whipping cream, 2 tablespoons instant chocolate or vanilla flavored pudding mix, and ¼ cup powdered sugar with an electric mixer on medium until soft peaks form. Beat in ⅔ cup chocolate-hazelnut spread until just combined.

*Note: If only one 15×10×1-inch baking pan is available, chill half the batter. As soon as the first cake is done, wash pan. Grease and line as for first cake. Volume of cake may be slightly less.

Per serving: 384 cal., 19 g total fat (8 g sat. fat), 41 mg chol., 280 mg sodium, 50 g carbo., 1 g fiber, 4 g pro.

Easy Bûche de Nöel

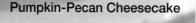

Pumpkin-Pecan Cheesecake

Pumpkin-Pecan Cheesecake

Pumpkin pie? Pecan pie? Cheesecake? Why not have them all in one divine confection baked in a gingersnap crust?

Prep: 30 minutes **Bake:** 40 minutes
Cool: 45 minutes **Chill:** 4 hours **Oven:** 350°F
Makes: 12 to 16 servings

½	cup graham cracker crumbs
¼	cup finely crushed gingersnaps
2	tablespoons finely chopped pecans
1	tablespoon all-purpose flour
1	tablespoon powdered sugar
2	tablespoons butter, melted
2	8-ounce packages cream cheese, softened
1	cup granulated sugar
4	eggs
1	15-ounce can pumpkin
¼	cup milk
½	teaspoon ground cinnamon
¼	teaspoon ground ginger
¼	teaspoon ground nutmeg
½	cup whipping cream
	Toasted pecan halves (see Note, page 17)

1. Preheat oven to 350°F. For crust, in a medium bowl combine graham cracker crumbs, crushed gingersnaps, the 2 tablespoons pecans, flour, powdered sugar, and melted butter. Press evenly onto the bottom of a 9-inch springform pan; set aside.

2. In a large mixing bowl beat cream cheese and granulated sugar with an electric mixer on medium speed until fluffy. Add 3 of the eggs, beating on low speed just until combined.

3. Place 1 cup of the cream cheese mixture in a medium mixing bowl. Add pumpkin, the remaining egg, the milk, cinnamon, ginger, and nutmeg. Beat on low speed just until combined. Pour pumpkin mixture into prepared pan. Top with cream cheese mixture. Use a knife or thin metal spatula to gently swirl through the layers to marble.

4. Place springform pan in a shallow baking pan. Bake for 40 to 45 minutes or until a 2½-inch area around the outside edge appears set when gently shaken. Cool on a wire rack for 15 minutes. Loosen crust from sides of pan. Cool 30 minutes more. Remove sides of pan. Cool completely. Cover and chill at least 4 hours or up to 3 days.

5. Just before serving, beat whipping cream until stiff peaks form. Top each serving with whipped cream and toasted pecans.

Per serving: 328 cal., 22 g total fat (13 g sat. fat), 131 mg chol., 209 mg sodium, 27 g carbo., 1 g fiber, 7 g pro.

Biscuit Bread Pudding with Lemon Sauce

Bread pudding, simultaneously soft, crunchy, sweet, rich, and fragrant with spices, takes on a new texture when made with biscuits rather than loaf bread.

Prep: 30 minutes **Bake:** 45 minutes
Stand: 10 minutes **Oven:** 350°F
Makes: 12 to 14 servings

9	cups coarsely crumbled homemade buttermilk biscuits (12 to 15 biscuits) or two 12-ounce packages refrigerated southern-style biscuits, baked according to package directions and crumbled
6	eggs, lightly beaten
2½	cups sugar
1	12-ounce can (1½ cups) evaporated milk
1	5-ounce can (⅔ cup) evaporated milk
⅓	cup butter, melted
1½	teaspoons vanilla
¾	teaspoon ground cinnamon
¾	teaspoon ground nutmeg
1	recipe Lemon Sauce

1. Preheat oven to 350°F. Place crumbled biscuits in a greased 13×9×2-inch baking dish. In a large bowl stir together eggs, sugar, evaporated milk, melted butter, vanilla, cinnamon, and nutmeg.

Pour egg mixture over biscuits, pressing to moisten evenly. Let stand for 10 minutes to thoroughly moisten biscuits.

2. Bake about 45 minutes or until a knife inserted near the center comes out clean. Serve warm with Lemon Sauce.

Lemon Sauce: In a medium saucepan stir together 2 lightly beaten eggs, ¼ cup water, and ¼ cup lemon juice. Add 1 cup sugar and ½ cup butter, cut up. Cook and stir until mixture is thickened and just bubbly on edges. If desired, strain sauce. Serve warm. Makes about 2 cups.

Per serving: 619 cal., 28 g total fat (13 g sat. fat), 187 mg chol., 719 mg sodium, 84 g carbo., 1 g fiber, 11 g pro.

Pumpkin-Filled Cream Puffs with Maple-Caramel Sauce

Clouds of spicy pumpkin mousse fill cream puffs that are drizzled with a rich sauce. What about the standard ice cream? Save it for another day.

Prep: 50 minutes **Bake:** 30 minutes
Cool: 10 minutes **Oven:** 400°F **Makes:** 8 servings

¾	**cup water**
⅓	**cup butter**
2	**teaspoons sugar**
⅛	**teaspoon salt**
¾	**cup all-purpose flour**
3	**eggs**
1	**recipe Pumpkin Mousse**
1	**recipe Maple-Caramel Sauce**
½	**cup coarsely chopped pecans, toasted (see Note, page 17)**

1. Preheat oven to 400°F. Line a large baking sheet with parchment paper; set aside. In a medium saucepan combine water, butter, sugar, and salt. Bring to boiling over medium heat. Add flour all at once, stirring vigorously with a wooden spoon. Cook and stir until mixture forms a ball and pulls away from the side of the pan. Remove from heat; cool for 10 minutes. Add eggs 1 at a time, beating well with a wooden spoon after each addition.

2. Drop 8 heaping tablespoons of dough 2 inches apart onto the prepared baking sheet. Bake for

30 to 35 minutes or until golden brown and firm. Transfer cream puffs to a wire rack and let cool.

3. Using a serrated knife, cut each cream puff in half horizontally; remove soft dough from inside. Fill cream puffs with Pumpkin Mousse. Replace tops. Spoon some of the warm Maple-Caramel Sauce onto eight dessert plates; sprinkle with some of the toasted pecans. Place a filled cream puff on top of the sauce on each plate. Drizzle each cream puff with remaining sauce and sprinkle with remaining pecans.

Pumpkin Mousse: In a chilled large mixing bowl beat 1 cup whipping cream, 3 tablespoons sugar, and 1 teaspoon pumpkin pie spice with the chilled beaters of an electric mixer on medium speed until soft peaks form (tips curl). Fold in 1 cup canned pumpkin. Cover and chill for up to 4 hours.

Maple-Caramel Sauce: In a small heavy saucepan stir together ½ cup packed brown sugar and 1 tablespoon cornstarch. Stir in ⅓ cup half-and-half or light cream, ¼ cup water, 2 tablespoons pure maple syrup, and 1 tablespoon butter. Cook and stir over medium heat until slightly thickened and bubbly (mixture may appear curdled before it bubbles). Cook and stir for 2 minutes more. Remove from heat; stir in ½ teaspoon vanilla. Serve warm.

Per serving: 417 cal., 28 g total fat (14 g sat. fat), 148 mg chol., 150 mg sodium, 38 g carbo., 2 g fiber, 6 g pro.

Pumpkin-Filled Cream Puffs with Maple-Caramel Sauce

Pumpkin Pistachio Cream Cannoli

These cannoli shells are filled with a luscious blend of ricotta, creamy mascarpone, pumpkin, fragrant spices, and pistachios to produce a dazzling holiday dessert.

Start to Finish: 25 minutes **Makes:** 12 servings

½   of an 8-ounce carton mascarpone cheese
¾   cup powdered sugar
¾   cup canned pumpkin
½   cup ricotta cheese
1   teaspoon pumpkin pie spice
½   cup chopped roasted pistachio nuts or toasted pecans (see Note, page 17)
½   cup whipping cream
12   purchased cannoli shells
     Powdered sugar

1. In a large bowl stir together mascarpone cheese, the ¾ cup powdered sugar, pumpkin, ricotta, and pumpkin pie spice until smooth. Stir in ¼ cup of the nuts; set aside.

2. In a chilled medium mixing bowl beat whipping cream until stiff peaks form; fold into pumpkin mixture. If desired, cover and chill up to 4 hours.

3. Spoon pumpkin mixture into a resealable plastic bag. Cut a ¾-inch hole in one corner of the bag. Pipe pumpkin mixture into cannoli shells, filling shells so pumpkin mixture is exposed on ends. Sprinkle ends of each cannoli with the remaining ¼ cup nuts. Arrange on serving platter; sprinkle with additional powdered sugar.

Per serving: 276 cal., 20 g total fat (7 g sat. fat), 31 mg chol., 29 mg sodium, 22 g carbo., 2 g fiber, 7 g pro.

Pumpkin Tiramisu

Chocolate and coffee syrup flavor traditional tiramisu, but this version counts on pumpkin, maple, and bourbon to add holiday appeal to this popular dessert.

Prep: 30 minutes **Chill:** 8 hours **Makes:** 6 servings

¼   cup pure maple syrup or maple-flavor syrup
1   tablespoon bourbon
1   3-ounce package ladyfingers, split
½   of a 15-ounce can (¾ cup) pumpkin
1   teaspoon ground cinnamon
½   teaspoon ground ginger
¼   teaspoon salt
1   cup whipping cream
¼   cup granulated sugar
½   of an 8-ounce carton mascarpone cheese
1   tablespoon powdered sugar
     Ground nutmeg

Pumpkin Pistachio
Cream Cannoli

1. Line a 9×5×3-inch loaf pan with plastic wrap; set aside. For syrup, in a small bowl combine maple syrup and bourbon. Arrange half of the ladyfingers in a single layer in the bottom of the prepared pan; drizzle evenly with half of the syrup.

2. For filling, in a small bowl combine pumpkin, cinnamon, ginger, and salt. In a small mixing bowl beat ½ cup of the whipping cream and granulated sugar with an electric mixer on medium speed until soft peaks form (tips curl). Gently fold whipped cream into pumpkin mixture.

3. In another small mixing bowl beat mascarpone cheese and powdered sugar on low speed until combined. Gradually beat in the remaining ½ cup whipping cream just until thickened (do not overbeat).

4. Evenly spread half of the filling over ladyfingers. Top with another layer of ladyfingers; drizzle with remaining syrup. Top with remaining filling. Drop spoonfuls of the mascarpone mixture over filling; spread evenly over filling with the back of the spoon. Cover and chill for 8 to 24 hours.

5. To serve, use the plastic wrap to lift tiramisu out of pan. Place on a serving platter; sprinkle with nutmeg. Cut crosswise into slices.

Per serving: 364 cal., 25 g total fat (15 g sat. fat), 110 mg chol., 147 mg sodium, 33 g carbo., 1 g fiber, 7 g pro.

Caramel Apple Trifle Parfaits

Toss cubes of spice cake, instead of sponge cake, with apple pie filling, toasted walnuts, raisins, and cream cheese for a swoon-worthy trifle triumph.

Prep: 45 minutes Bake: per package directions
Makes: 8 servings

- 1 package 2-layer-size spice cake mix
- 1 8-ounce package cream cheese, softened
- 1 12.25-ounce jar caramel-flavor ice cream topping
- 1½ cups whipping cream
- 1 21-ounce can apple pie filling
- ⅔ cup chopped walnuts, toasted (see Note, page 17)
- ½ cup golden raisins (optional)

Pumpkin Tiramisu

1. Prepare and bake cake mix according to package directions for a 13×9×2-inch baking pan. Cool cake thoroughly in pan on a wire rack.

2. Cut half of the cake into 1-inch cubes (you should have 8 cups); set aside. Reserve remaining cake for another use.

3. In a large mixing bowl beat cream cheese with an electric mixer on medium speed until light and fluffy. Slowly add ice cream topping, beating on low speed just until combined. In a medium mixing bowl beat whipping cream until stiff peaks form; fold whipped cream into cream cheese mixture.

4. In each of eight 14-ounce stemmed glasses or tumblers, spoon 2 rounded tablespoons of the whipped cream mixture. Top with ½ cup cake cubes and another 2 rounded tablespoons of the whipped cream mixture. Top with ¼ cup of the apple pie filling. Sprinkle walnuts and, if desired, raisins over pie filling. Add another ½ cup cake cubes and remaining whipped cream mixture. Serve immediately or cover and chill for up to 4 hours.

Per serving: 803 cal., 38 g total fat (19 g sat. fat), 93 mg chol., 670 mg sodium, 108 g carbo., 2 g fiber, 6 g pro.

sugar and spice

Confections of every kind are welcome at the holidays! The selection here features a mass of favorites, from fudge to brittle and truffles to shortbread. They will satisfy your need for the familiar and for surprise.

Toffee Jan Hagels,
page 107

Pumpkin Pie Drops

*When a piece of pie is too much, serve cookies!
Their aroma and taste are just like pie and much
easier to tote and share.*

Prep: 30 minutes **Bake:** 10 minutes per batch
Oven: 375°F **Makes:** about 48 cookies

1	cup butter, softened
½	cup granulated sugar
½	cup packed brown sugar
2	teaspoons pumpkin pie spice
1	teaspoon baking powder
½	teaspoon baking soda
¼	teaspoon salt
1	egg
1	cup canned pumpkin
1	to 2 tablespoons finely chopped crystallized ginger
2	cups all-purpose flour
½	cup chopped almonds, toasted (see Note, page 17) (optional)
1	recipe Brown Butter Icing
	Chopped almonds, toasted (optional)
	Finely chopped crystallized ginger (optional)

1. Preheat oven to 375°F. In a large mixing bowl beat butter with an electric mixer on medium to high speed for 30 seconds. Add granulated sugar, brown sugar, pumpkin pie spice, baking powder, baking soda, and salt. Beat until combined, scraping sides of bowl occasionally. Beat in egg, pumpkin, and the 1 to 2 tablespoons crystallized ginger. Beat in as much of the flour as you can with the mixer. Stir in any remaining flour and, if desired, the ½ cup almonds.

2. Drop dough by rounded teaspoons 2 inches apart onto an ungreased cookie sheet. Bake for 10 to 12 minutes or until bottoms are light brown. Transfer to a wire rack and let cool.

3. Place Brown Butter Icing in a heavy plastic bag. Cut a small hole in one corner of the bag and drizzle icing over cookies. If desired, sprinkle cookies with additional chopped almonds and crystallized ginger, pressing lightly into icing. Let cookies stand until icing sets.

Brown Butter Icing: In a medium saucepan heat ⅓ cup butter over low heat until butter turns the color of light brown sugar, stirring frequently. Remove saucepan from heat. Slowly beat in 2½ cups powdered sugar, 1 teaspoon vanilla, and enough milk (2 to 3 tablespoons) to make drizzling consistency.

Pumpkin Pie Drops

Per cookie: 110 cal., 5 g total fat (3 g sat. fat), 18 mg chol., 72 mg sodium, 15 g carbo., 0 g fiber, 1 g pro.

Cherry Chocolate Chip Cookies

Tart dried cherries, snipped into chewy bits, join semisweet chocolate in a cookie blend that is sure to win rave reviews.

Prep: 25 minutes **Bake:** 9 minutes per batch
Oven: 375°F **Makes:** about 48 cookies

- 1 cup butter, softened
- 1 cup granulated sugar
- 1 cup packed brown sugar
- 1 teaspoon baking soda
- 1 teaspoon salt
- 2 eggs
- 1½ teaspoons vanilla
- 3 cups all-purpose flour
- 1 12-ounce package semisweet chocolate pieces
- 1 cup snipped dried cherries

1. Preheat oven to 375°F. In a large mixing bowl beat butter with an electric mixer on medium to high speed for 30 seconds. Add granulated sugar, brown sugar, baking soda, and salt. Beat until combined, scraping sides of bowl occasionally. Beat in eggs and vanilla until combined. Beat in as much of the flour as you can with the mixer. Stir in any remaining flour. Stir in chocolate pieces and cherries.

2. Drop dough by tablespoons 2 inches apart onto an ungreased cookie sheet. Bake about 9 minutes or until edges are light brown. Transfer to a wire rack and let cool.

Per cookie: 136 cal., 6 g total fat (4 g sat. fat), 19 mg chol., 206 mg sodium, 20 g carbo., 1 g fiber, 2 g pro.

Almond Butter Blossoms

Familiar chocolate kiss-topped peanut butter cookies take on a different taste and a lighter hue when made with decadent almond butter.

Prep: 30 minutes **Bake:** 8 minutes per batch
Oven: 350°F **Makes:** about 48 cookies

- ½ cup butter, softened
- ½ cup almond butter
- ½ cup granulated sugar
- ½ cup packed brown sugar

Almond Butter Blossoms

- ¾ teaspoon baking soda
- ½ teaspoon cream of tartar
- ¼ teaspoon salt
- 1 egg
- 2 tablespoons milk
- ½ teaspoon vanilla
- 1 cup whole wheat flour
- 1 cup all-purpose flour
- 3 tablespoons granulated sugar
- 2 tablespoons finely ground almonds
- 48 milk chocolate kisses with almonds

1. Preheat oven to 350°F. In a large mixing bowl beat butter and almond butter with an electric mixer on medium to high speed for 30 seconds. Add the ½ cup granulated sugar, brown sugar, baking soda, cream of tartar, and salt. Beat until combined, scraping bowl occasionally. Beat in egg, milk, and vanilla until combined. Beat in whole wheat flour and as much of the all-purpose flour as you can with the mixer. Stir in any remaining flour.

2. In a small bowl combine the 3 tablespoons granulated sugar and almonds. Shape dough into 1-inch balls. Roll balls in sugar-almond mixture to coat. Place balls 2 inches apart on an ungreased cookie sheet.

3. Bake for 8 to 10 minutes or until edges are firm and tops crack. Immediately press a chocolate kiss into the center of each cookie. Transfer to a wire rack and let cool.

Per cookie: 101 cal., 5 g total fat (2 g sat. fat), 11 mg chol., 52 mg sodium, 12 g carbo., 1 g fiber, 2 g pro.

Orange-Sugared
Snowballs

4. Bake for 12 to 14 minutes or until bottoms are light brown. Cool on cookie sheet for 2 minutes. Roll cookies in the sugar-orange peel mixture again while still warm. Transfer to a wire rack and let cool.

Per cookie: 126 cal., 6 g total fat (4 g sat. fat), 16 mg chol., 44 mg sodium, 17 g carbo., g fiber, 1 g pro.

Ginger Crinkles

Cracked-top cookies are often chocolate, but not these. This holiday cookie features fragrant ground ginger in its dough and finely chopped crystallized ginger on top. What's more, they fill a kitchen with that home-sweet-home aroma.

Prep: 30 minutes **Bake:** 8 minutes per batch
Oven: 375°F **Makes:** about 32 cookies

¾	cup butter, softened
1	cup granulated sugar
1	teaspoon baking powder
1	teaspoon baking soda
2	teaspoons grated fresh ginger*
½	teaspoon ground cinnamon
½	teaspoon ground cloves
¼	teaspoon salt
1	egg
¼	cup molasses
2⅔	cups all-purpose flour
½	cup coarse sugar
¼	cup finely chopped crystallized ginger (optional)

1. Preheat oven to 375°F. In a large mixing bowl beat butter with an electric mixer on medium to high speed for 30 seconds. Add granulated sugar, baking powder, baking soda, fresh ginger, cinnamon, cloves, and salt. Beat until combined, scraping sides of bowl occasionally. Beat in egg and molasses until combined. Beat in as much of the flour as you can with the mixer. Stir in any remaining flour.

2. Shape dough into 1-inch balls. In a small bowl combine the coarse sugar and, if desired, the crystallized ginger. Roll balls in sugar mixture to coat. Place balls 2 inches apart on an ungreased cookie sheet.

Orange-Sugared Snowballs

Orange peel and orange juice give buttery sandie-style cookies a tangy infusion of fresh citrus flavors.

Prep: 20 minutes **Bake:** 12 minutes per batch
Oven: 325°F **Makes:** about 30 cookies

¾	cup granulated sugar
2	teaspoons finely shredded orange peel
1	tablespoon finely shredded orange peel
1	cup butter, softened
¾	cup powdered sugar
1	tablespoon orange juice
2⅔	cups all-purpose flour

1. In a food processor or blender combine the granulated sugar and the 2 teaspoons orange peel. Cover and process or blend until well combined; set aside.

2. Preheat oven to 325°F. In a large mixing bowl beat butter with an electric mixer on medium to high speed for 30 seconds. Add powdered sugar. Beat until combined, scraping sides of bowl occasionally. Beat in the orange juice until combined. Beat in as much of the flour as you can. Stir in any remaining flour and the 1 tablespoon orange peel.

3. Shape dough into 1¼-inch balls. Roll balls in the sugar-orange peel mixture to coat. Place balls 2 inches apart on an ungreased cookie sheet.

3. Bake about 8 minutes or until edges are set and tops are crackled. Cool on cookie sheet for 1 minute. Transfer to a wire rack and let cool.

*Note: If you don't want to use crystallized ginger in the sugar mixture, increase the grated fresh ginger in the dough to 1 tablespoon.

Per cookie: 123 cal., 5 g total fat (2 g sat. fat), 18 mg chol., 103 mg sodium, 19 g carbo., 0 g fiber, 1 g pro.

Chocolate-Caramel Thumbprints

Roll a chocolate dough in pecans, make a thumbprint in the center, and fill it with a dab of luscious caramel as a takeoff on the butter-walnut-jam-filled versions.

Prep: 30 minutes **Bake:** 10 minutes per batch
Chill: 2 hours **Oven:** 350°F
Makes: about 36 cookies

1	egg
½	cup butter, softened
⅔	cup sugar
2	tablespoons milk
1	teaspoon vanilla
1	cup all-purpose flour
⅓	cup unsweetened cocoa powder
¼	teaspoon salt
16	vanilla caramels, unwrapped
3	tablespoons whipping cream
1¼	cups finely chopped pecans
½	cup semisweet chocolate pieces
1	teaspoon shortening

1. Separate egg. Cover and chill egg white until needed. Set yolk aside.

2. In a large mixing bowl beat butter with an electric mixer on medium to high speed for 30 seconds. Add sugar and beat well. Beat in the egg yolk, milk, and vanilla.

3. In a medium bowl stir together the flour, cocoa powder, and salt. Add flour mixture to butter mixture and beat until well combined. Wrap cookie dough in plastic wrap and chill about 2 hours or until easy to handle.

4. Preheat oven to 350°F. Lightly grease a cookie sheet; set aside. In a small saucepan heat and stir caramels and whipping cream over low heat until mixture is smooth. Set aside.

5. Lightly beat the egg white with a fork. Shape dough into 1-inch balls. Roll balls in egg white, then roll in nuts to coat. Place balls 1 inch apart on prepared cookie sheet. Using your thumb, make an indentation in the center of each ball.

6. Bake about 10 minutes or until edges are firm. Spoon some of the melted caramel mixture into cookie centers. (If necessary, reheat caramel mixture if it hardens.) Transfer cookies to a wire rack and let cool.

7. In another small saucepan heat and stir chocolate pieces and shortening over low heat until chocolate melts and mixture is smooth. Cool slightly. Drizzle chocolate mixture over tops of cookies. Let stand until chocolate is set.

Per cookie: 114 cal., 7 g total fat (3 g sat. fat), 14 mg chol., 48 mg sodium, 12 g carbo., 1 g fiber, 1 g pro.

Chocolate-Caramel
Thumbprints

Praline Snickerdoodles

Mysterious, tangy snickerdoodles get a double, nutty dimension when toffee pieces and chopped pecans join the dough.

Prep: 30 minutes **Bake:** 10 minutes per batch
Chill: 1 hour **Oven:** 375°F **Makes:** about 48 cookies

1	cup butter, softened
1¾	cups sugar
1	teaspoon cream of tartar
1	teaspoon baking soda
¼	teaspoon salt
2	eggs
1	teaspoon vanilla
3	cups all-purpose flour
1	cup toffee pieces
½	cup chopped pecans
2	teaspoons ground cinnamon

1. In a large mixing bowl beat butter with an electric mixer on medium to high speed for 30 seconds. Add 1½ cups of the sugar, cream of tartar, baking soda, and salt. Beat until combined, scraping sides of bowl occasionally. Beat in eggs and vanilla until combined. Beat in as much of the flour as you can with the mixer. Stir in any remaining flour, the toffee pieces, and pecans. Cover and chill dough about 1 hour or until easy to handle.

2. Preheat oven to 375°F. In a small bowl stir together the remaining ¼ cup sugar and the cinnamon. Shape dough into 1½-inch balls. Roll balls in sugar mixture to coat. Place balls 2 inches apart on an ungreased cookie sheet. Bake for 10 to 12 minutes or until edges are golden brown. Transfer to a wire rack and let cool.

Per cookie: 126 cal., 6 g total fat (3 g sat. fat), 20 mg chol., 79 mg sodium, 16 g carbo., 0 g fiber, 2 g pro.

Chocolate Cream Spritz

Melt-in-your-mouth butter spritz cookies become even more irresistible with the addition of rich, creamy mascarpone cheese and cocoa powder.

Prep: 25 minutes **Bake:** 8 minutes per batch
Oven: 375°F **Makes:** about 84 cookies

1½	cups butter, softened
½	of an 8-ounce carton mascarpone cheese or ½ of an 8-ounce package cream cheese, softened
½	cup granulated sugar
½	cup packed brown sugar
¼	cup unsweetened cocoa powder
1	teaspoon baking powder
2	egg yolks or 1 egg
1	teaspoon vanilla
3¼	cups all-purpose flour

1. Preheat oven to 375°F. In a large mixing bowl beat butter and mascarpone cheese with an electric mixer on medium to high speed for 30 seconds. Add granulated sugar, brown sugar, cocoa powder, and baking powder. Beat until combined, scraping sides of bowl occasionally.

2. Beat in egg yolks and vanilla. Beat in as much of the flour as you can with mixer. Stir in any remaining flour.

3. Force unchilled dough through a cookie press onto an ungreased cookie sheet. Bake for 8 to 10 minutes or until edges are firm. Transfer to a wire rack and let cool.

Per cookie: 65 cal., 2 g total fat (2 g sat. fat), 16 mg chol., 29 mg sodium, 6 g carbo., 0 g fiber, 1 g pro.

Eggnog Kringla

Eggnog's rich, spiced flavor is an especially fitting addition to this classic melt-in-your-mouth Norwegian cookie.

Prep: 30 minutes **Bake:** 5 minutes per batch
Chill: 6 hours **Oven:** 425°F **Makes:** 40 cookies

½	cup butter, softened
¾	cup sugar
1	teaspoon baking powder
1	teaspoon baking soda
½	teaspoon ground nutmeg
¼	teaspoon salt
1	egg
½	teaspoon vanilla
3	cups all-purpose flour
¾	cup dairy eggnog
	Powdered sugar

Eggnog Kringla

1. In a large mixing bowl beat butter with an electric mixer on medium to high speed for 30 seconds. Beat in the sugar, scraping sides of bowl occasionally. Beat in baking powder, baking soda, nutmeg and salt until combined. Beat in egg and vanilla until combined. Alternately add flour and eggnog, beating after each addition until combined. Cover and chill dough at least 6 hours or overnight.

2. Preheat oven to 425°F. Divide dough in half. On a floured surface, roll each dough half into a 10×5-inch rectangle. With a sharp knife, cut each rectangle into twenty 5×½-inch strips. Roll each strip into a 10-inch rope. Shape into a loop, crossing 1½ inches from ends. Twist rope at crossing point. Lift loop over ends and seal, forming a pretzel shape. Place on an ungreased baking sheet.

3. Bake about 5 minutes or until very light brown. Transfer to a wire rack and let cool. Sprinkle with powdered sugar.

Per cookie: 81 cal., 3 g total fat (2 g sat. fat), 14 mg chol., 76 mg sodium, 12 g carbo., 0 g fiber, 1 g pro.

Chocolate-Nut Spirals

Prep: 30 minutes **Bake:** 7 minutes per batch
Chill: 2 hours **Oven:** 375°F **Makes:** about 48 cookies

- 1 **16-ounce roll refrigerated sugar cookie dough**
- 2 **tablespoons unsweetened cocoa powder**
- 2 **tablespoons all-purpose flour**
- ½ **cup finely chopped honey-roasted peanuts or toffee pieces**
- 1 **tablespoon coarse sugar**

1. Divide cookie dough in half. In a resealable plastic bag combine half of the dough with the cocoa powder. In another resealable plastic bag combine the other half of the dough with the flour. Seal bags; knead with your hands until combined.

2. Place chocolate dough between two pieces of waxed paper. Place white dough between two more pieces of waxed paper. Roll each dough portion into a 12×6-inch rectangle. Remove top pieces of waxed paper. Sprinkle peanuts evenly over chocolate dough. Using waxed paper, invert white dough on top of chocolate dough; press gently to seal. Remove waxed paper that is now on top.

3. Beginning with a long side, carefully roll up doughs, using remaining waxed paper to lift and guide the roll. Pinch edges to seal. Roll log in coarse sugar to coat. Wrap log in plastic wrap; chill for 2 to 4 hours or until log is firm enough to slice.

4. Preheat oven to 375°F. Cut log into ¼-inch-thick slices. Place slices 2 inches apart on an ungreased cookie sheet. Bake for 7 to 9 minutes or until edges are just firm. Transfer to a wire rack and let cool.

Per cookie: 50 cal., 2 g total fat (1 g sat. fat), 3 mg chol., 44 mg sodium, 7 g carbo., 0 g fiber, 1 g pro.

Chocolate Gingerbread People

Prep: 40 minutes **Bake:** 6 minutes per batch
Oven: 350°F **Makes:** about 48 cookies

- ½ **cup butter, softened**
- 6 **ounces bittersweet or semisweet chocolate, melted and cooled**
- ⅔ **cup granulated sugar**
- ½ **cup packed brown sugar**
- 1 **teaspoon ground ginger**
- ¾ **teaspoon baking soda**
- ½ **teaspoon salt**
- ½ **teaspoon ground cinnamon**
- ¼ **teaspoon ground cloves**
- 1 **egg**
- 1¾ **cups all-purpose flour**
- 1 **recipe Powdered Sugar Icing (page 151)
Decorative sprinkles or candies (optional)**

1. In a large mixing bowl beat butter with an electric mixer on medium to high speed for 30 seconds. Beat in the chocolate, granulated sugar, brown sugar, ginger, baking soda, salt, cinnamon and cloves, scraping bowl. Beat in egg until combined. Beat in as much of the flour as you can. Stir in any remaining flour. Divide dough in half.

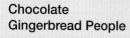

Chocolate
Gingerbread People

104

2. Preheat oven to 350°F. Lightly grease or line cookie sheets with parchment paper; set aside. On a lightly floured surface, roll half of the dough at a time until ⅛ inch thick. Using a 2½- to 3-inch people-shape cookie cutter, cut out dough, rerolling scraps as necessary. Place 1 inch apart on prepared cookie sheets.

3. Bake for 6 to 8 minutes or until edges are set. Cool on cookie sheets for 1 minute. Transfer to wire racks and let cool. Decorate cookies with Powdered Sugar Icing. If desired, before icing dries, sprinkle with decorative sprinkles or candies.

Per cookie: 83 cal., 3 g total fat (2 g sat. fat), 10 mg chol., 60 mg sodium, 13 g carbo., 0 g fiber, 1 g pro.

Molded Gingersnap Shortbread

Ginger, cinnamon, cloves, and molasses give classic shortbread cookies a gingerbread flair. These are fun to make in wedges or pressed into shortbread molds.

Prep: 30 minutes **Bake:** 18 minutes **Oven:** 325°F
Makes: 16 to 18 cookies

2	cups all-purpose flour
½	cup powdered sugar
¼	teaspoon ground ginger
¼	teaspoon ground cinnamon
⅛	teaspoon ground cloves
1	cup cold butter
2	tablespoons molasses
	Nonstick cooking spray
	Granulated sugar (optional)

1. Preheat oven to 325°F. In a large bowl combine flour, powdered sugar, ginger, cinnamon, and cloves. Using a pastry blender, cut in butter, along with the molasses, until mixture resembles fine crumbs. Knead mixture until it forms a ball.

2. Lightly coat a 7½- to 8-inch shortbread mold with cooking spray; dust with flour. Press half of the dough at a time into the prepared mold, flouring the mold between uses. Unmold dough onto a very large ungreased cookie sheet; trim edges if necessary. (Or flatten dough into two 8-inch circles on one very large ungreased cookie sheet or two smaller cookie sheets. Use your fingers to make a scalloped edge on each circle. Sprinkle each circle with granulated sugar.) Do not sprinkle molded cookies with sugar.

3. Bake for 18 to 20 minutes until bottoms just start to turn golden brown and centers are set. Cut molded shortbread into nine pieces while warm. (Or cut each circle into eight wedges awhile warm.) Cool on cookie sheet for 5 minutes. Transfer to a wire rack and let cool.

Per cookie: 181 cal., 12 g total fat (7 g sat. fat), 31 mg chol., 83 mg sodium, 18 g carbo., 0 g fiber, 2 g pro.

Cherry-Rum Biscotti

Biscotti, the twice-baked cookie that fans love to dunk in coffee or milk, features rum-soaked cherries and a drizzle of rum-soaked icing.

Prep: 30 minutes **Bake:** 40 minutes
Stand: 15 minutes **Cool:** 1 hour **Oven:** 350°F/300°F
Makes: about 48 cookies

1¼	cups dried tart red cherries, coarsely chopped
½	cup light rum or spiced rum
½	cup butter, softened
1	cup sugar
1	tablespoon baking powder
¼	teaspoon salt
3	eggs
½	teaspoon vanilla
3¼	cups all-purpose flour
¾	cup chopped pecans, toasted (see Note, page 17)
1	recipe Rum Icing

1. In a small saucepan combine cherries and rum. Bring just to simmering over medium heat. Remove from heat; let stand 15 minutes. Drain well, reserving rum for the icing and pressing cherries to remove excess liquid. Set cherries aside.

2. Preheat oven to 350°F. Lightly grease a very large cookie sheet; set aside. In a large mixing bowl beat butter with an electric mixer on medium to high speed for 30 seconds. Add sugar, baking powder, and salt. Beat until combined, scraping sides of bowl occasionally. Beat in eggs and vanilla until combined. Beat in as much of the flour as you can with the mixer. Stir in any remaining flour, the drained cherries, and pecans.

3. Divide dough into thirds. Shape each dough portion into a 9-inch-long loaf. Place loaves 3 inches apart on prepared cookie sheet; flatten each roll slightly until about 2½ inches wide. Bake for 20 to 25 minutes or until golden brown and tops are cracked. Cool on cookie sheet for 1 hour.

4. Preheat oven to 300°F. Transfer baked loaves to a cutting board. Use a serrated knife to cut each loaf diagonally into ½-inch slices.

5. Place slices, cut sides down, on an ungreased cookie sheet. Bake for 10 minutes. Turn slices over; bake for 10 to 15 minutes more or until crisp and dry. Transfer cookies to a wire rack and let cool. Drizzle with Rum Icing. Let stand until icing is set.

Rum Icing: In a small bowl stir together 1½ cups powdered sugar and 1 tablespoon of the reserved rum. Add enough additional rum (1 to 2 tablespoons) to make drizzling consistency.

Per cookie: 115 cal., 4 g total fat (1 g sat. fat), 18 mg chol., 55 mg sodium, 18 g carbo., 1 g fiber, 1 g pro.

Cherry-Rum Biscotti

Toffee
Jan Hagels

Whole Wheat Gingerbread Bars with Maple Frosting

Swap white flour for whole wheat in this sumptuous sweet. Instead of topping it with lemon sauce or powdered sugar, frost it with festive maple frosting.

Prep: 20 minutes **Bake:** 25 minutes **Oven:** 375°F
Makes: 36 bars

- ½ cup shortening
- 1 cup all-purpose flour
- ½ cup whole wheat flour
- ½ cup molasses
- ½ cup hot water
- ¼ cup packed brown sugar
- 1 egg
- ¾ teaspoon baking powder
- ¾ teaspoon ground cinnamon
- ½ teaspoon ground ginger
- ¼ teaspoon baking soda
- ¼ teaspoon salt
- ½ cup chopped walnuts
- 1 recipe Maple Frosting

1. Preheat oven to 375°F. Lightly grease a 13×9×2-inch baking pan; set pan aside. In a mixing bowl beat shortening with an electric mixer on medium to high speed about 30 seconds or until softened. Add all-purpose flour, whole wheat flour, molasses, hot water, brown sugar, egg, baking powder, cinnamon, ginger, baking soda, and salt. Beat until combined, scraping sides of bowl occasionally. Stir in walnuts.

2. Spread batter in prepared pan. Bake about 25 minutes or until a toothpick inserted in center comes out clean. Cool in pan on a wire rack. Frost with Maple Frosting. Cut into bars.

Maple Frosting: In a large mixing bowl beat ⅓ cup softened butter until fluffy. Slowly add 2 cups powdered sugar, beating well. Beat in ¼ cup milk and ½ teaspoon maple flavoring. Gradually beat in 2½ cups additional powdered sugar. Beat in a little additional milk, if needed, to make spreading consistency.

Per bar: 149 cal., 6 g total fat (2 g sat. fat), 11 mg chol., 50 mg sodium, 24 g carbo., 0 g fiber, 1 g pro.

Toffee Jan Hagels

Cut in pointed diamond shapes and drizzled with chocolate, these cookies offer a fresh shape and rich flavor on a cookie-candy display.

Prep: 20 minutes **Bake:** 20 minutes
Cool: 10 minutes **Oven:** 350°F **Makes:** about 48 bars

- 1 cup butter, softened
- 1 cup packed brown sugar
- ½ teaspoon ground cinnamon
- ¼ teaspoon salt
- 2 eggs
- 1 teaspoon vanilla
- 2 cups all-purpose flour
- ½ cup sliced almonds
- ½ cup toffee pieces
- ½ cup semisweet chocolate pieces
- 1 teaspoon shortening

1. Preheat oven to 350°F. Lightly grease a 15×10×1-inch baking pan; set aside. Beat butter with an electric mixer on medium speed for 30 seconds. Beat in the brown sugar, cinnamon, and salt until combined, scraping bowl. Beat in eggs and vanilla until combined. Beat in as much of the flour as you can. Stir in any remaining flour.

2. Spread batter evenly in prepared pan; sprinkle evenly with almonds and toffee pieces. Bake about 20 minutes or until firm and light brown. Cool in pan on a wire rack for 10 minutes. Cut into 1½-inch diamonds while still warm.

3. Melt chocolate pieces and shortening over low heat until smooth. Cool slightly. Transfer chocolate mixture to a heavy plastic bag. Cut a small hole in one corner of the bag and drizzle over bars. Let stand until chocolate sets.

Per bar: 100 cal., 6 g total fat (3 g sat. fat), 19 mg chol., 49 mg sodium, 11 g carbo., 0 g fiber, 1 g pro.

Golden Fruitcake Bars

Forget making the fruitcake and letting it stand for days if not weeks. This recipe produces fruitcake in a fraction of the time and yields bars instead of loaves.

Prep: 30 minutes **Bake:** 25 minutes **Stand:** 1 hour
Cool: 10 minutes **Oven:** 350°F **Makes:** 42 bars

- 1 cup golden raisins, coarsely chopped
- 1 cup dried cranberries, coarsely chopped
- 1 cup dried apricots, finely snipped
- 1 cup brandy or orange juice
- 1 16-ounce package pound cake mix
- ½ cup lightly salted, dry-roasted pistachio nuts, chopped
- 1 cup powdered sugar

1. In a medium bowl combine raisins, cranberries, apricots, and brandy. Cover and let stand for 1 hour or overnight. Drain well, reserving brandy.

2. Preheat oven to 350°F. Grease a 15×10×1-inch baking pan; set pan aside. Prepare pound cake mix according to the package directions, except add one additional egg. Fold the drained fruit and pistachio nuts into the cake batter. Spread batter in prepared pan (pan will be very full).

3. Bake for 25 to 30 minutes until bars are golden on top and a toothpick inserted in the center comes out clean. Cool in pan on a wire rack for 10 minutes.

4. Meanwhile, for icing, in a small bowl combine powdered sugar and 2 tablespoons of the reserved brandy. Stir in additional brandy, 1 teaspoon at a time, to make drizzling consistency. Drizzle icing over warm bars. Cool completely. Cut into bars.

Per bar: 113 cal., 2 g total fat (1 g sat. fat), 16 mg chol., 48 mg sodium, 19 g carbo., 1 g fiber, 1 g pro.

Caramel Corn Party Mix

A little sweet, a little spicy, and totally irresistible, this mix combines the best of two seasonal favorites: caramel corn and cereal mix. A great choice for an afternoon gathering or a big game.

Prep: 15 minutes **Bake:** 20 minutes **Oven:** 300°F
Makes: 8 cups mix

- 4 cups popped popcorn
- 2 cups bite-size wheat or bran square cereal
- 1½ cups small pretzels or pretzel sticks
- 1½ cups pecan halves
- ¾ cup packed brown sugar
- ⅓ cup butter
- 3 tablespoons light-color corn syrup
- 1 teaspoon pumpkin pie spice
- ¼ teaspoon baking soda
- ¼ teaspoon vanilla
  Dash cayenne pepper

1. Preheat oven to 300°F. Remove all unpopped kernels from popped popcorn. Combine popcorn, cereal, pretzels, and pecans in a 17×12×2-inch baking pan or roasting pan.

Golden Fruitcake Bars

2. In a medium saucepan combine brown sugar, butter, and corn syrup. Cook and stir over medium heat until mixture boils; reduce heat to medium-low. Cook, without stirring, for 5 minutes more. Remove from heat; stir in pumpkin pie spice, baking soda, vanilla, and cayenne pepper. Pour over popcorn mixture in pan, stirring gently to coat.

3. Bake for 15 minutes; stir popcorn mixture and bake 5 minutes more. Spread on a large piece of buttered foil to cool. Break into pieces. Store tightly covered for up to 1 week.

Per ½ cup: 197 cal., 12 g total fat (3 g sat. fat), 11 mg chol., 172 mg sodium, 23 g carbo., 2 g fiber, 2 g pro.

Caramel Corn Party Mix

Dark Chocolate Butter Toffee
Drizzles of bitter chocolate and white chocolate dress up pieces of classic toffee candy. Pretty to serve, pretty to give.

Prep: 15 minutes **Cook:** 10 minutes
Stand: 30 minutes **Chill:** 40 minutes
Makes: about 2¼ pounds (24 servings)

1	cup unsalted butter, cut cup
1½	cups sugar
2	tablespoons water
1	tablespoon light-color corn syrup
1¼	cups finely chopped pecans
12	ounces bittersweet chocolate, chopped
2	ounces vanilla-flavor candy coating

1. Line a 15×10×1-inch baking pan with foil, extending foil over edges of pan; set pan aside. Butter the sides of a 2-quart heavy saucepan. In saucepan melt butter; add the sugar, water, and corn syrup. Cook and stir over medium-high heat until mixture boils. Clip a candy thermometer to side of pan.

2. Reduce heat to medium; continue boiling at a moderate, steady rate, stirring frequently, until thermometer registers 290°F, soft-crack stage (about 10 minutes). (Adjust heat as necessary to maintain a steady boil.) Remove saucepan from heat; remove thermometer. Carefully stir in 1 cup of the pecans. Quickly pour candy into prepared pan, spreading to edges. Let stand in pan on a wire rack about 30 minutes or until set.

3. Meanwhile, place half of the bittersweet chocolate in a microwave-safe bowl. Microwave, uncovered, on 100 percent power (high) for 1 minute; stir until smooth. Spread melted chocolate over top of cooled toffee. Chill about 20 minutes or until firm.

4. When firm, use foil to lift candy out of pan; turn candy over onto a sheet of waxed paper; remove foil. Microwave the remaining bittersweet chocolate, uncovered, on 100 percent power (high) for 1 minute; stir until smooth. Spread melted chocolate over top of toffee; sprinkle with the remaining ¼ cup pecans.

5. Place candy coating in a microwave-safe bowl. Microwave, uncovered, on 100 percent power (high) about 2 minutes or until melted, stirring every 30 seconds. Cool slightly. Transfer to a small, heavy plastic bag. Cut a small hole in one corner of the bag and drizzle over toffee. Chill 20 minutes or until set.

6. When set, break toffee into pieces. Cover tightly and chill for up to 3 weeks.

Per serving: 189 cal., 13 g total fat (7 g sat. fat), 17 mg chol., 4 mg sodium, 18 g carbo., 1 g fiber, 2 g pro.

Mixed-Nut Brittle

Rum-Raisin Clusters

Nut-only clusters give way to a fruity tweak as raisins or cherries join chopped pecans and rum in creamy chocolate.

Prep: 15 minutes **Chill:** 30 minutes
Makes: about 48 clusters

- 12 ounces semisweet chocolate, chopped
- ⅓ cup whipping cream
- 2 tablespoons spiced rum
- 1 teaspoon finely shredded orange peel
- 2 cups raisins or dried tart cherries
- 1 cup chopped pecans, toasted

1. Line a large baking sheet with waxed paper; set aside. In a medium heavy saucepan heat and stir chocolate, whipping cream, rum, and orange peel over low heat until chocolate melts and mixture is smooth. Stir in raisins and pecans.

2. Drop chocolate mixture by teaspoonfuls onto prepared baking sheet. Chill, uncovered, about 30 minutes or until set. (Or spoon chocolate mixture into foil candy cups placed in a miniature muffin tin for support.) Cover and chill for up to 1 week or freeze for up to 3 months.

Per cluster: 75 cal., 4 g total fat (2 g sat. fat), 2 mg chol., 2 mg sodium, 10 g carbo., 1 g fiber, 1 g pro.

Mixed-Nut Brittle

For a bit of variety, let walnuts, cashews, almonds, and other nuts join peanuts in brittle making.

Start to Finish: 15 minutes **Makes:** 16 servings

- ½ cup sugar
- ½ cup light-color corn syrup
- ½ cup salted mixed nuts
- 1 tablespoon butter
- ½ teaspoon vanilla
- ½ teaspoon baking soda

1. Grease a small baking sheet; set aside. In a microwave-safe 4-cup glass measuring cup combine sugar and corn syrup. Microwave, uncovered, on 100 percent power (high) 5 minutes, stirring twice.

2. Stir in nuts and butter. Microwave, uncovered, on 100 percent power (high) for 1 to 2 minutes more or just until mixture turns golden (mixture continues to cook and becomes more golden when removed from the microwave).

3. Stir in vanilla and baking soda. Immediately pour mixture onto prepared baking sheet. Use two forks to lift and pull brittle into a thin sheet as it cools (this helps make the brittle crisp). Cool completely; break into irregular pieces. Store tightly covered at room temperature up to 1 week.

Per serving: 89 cal., 3 g total fat (1 g sat. fat), 1 mg chol., 72 mg sodium, 15 g carbo., 0 g fiber, 1 g pro.

Mocha Truffles

Choose dark baking chocolate and slip in coffee liqueur for these sophisticated truffles.

Prep: 45 minutes **Stand:** 5 minutes **Chill:** 3 hours
Freeze: 30 minutes **Makes:** about 48 truffles

- ¾ **cup whipping cream**
- 2 **tablespoons butter**
- 14 **ounces premium dark baking chocolate, chopped**
- 1 **tablespoon coffee liqueur**
- 15 **ounces white baking chocolate, chopped**
- 1 **tablespoon shortening**
- 1 **tablespoon instant coffee crystals**

1. In a medium saucepan heat whipping cream and butter over medium heat just to boiling. Remove saucepan from heat. Add dark chocolate, but do not stir. Cover and let stand at room temperature for 5 minutes. Stir until smooth. Stir in coffee liqueur. Cover and chill for 1½ to 2 hours or until almost firm, stirring once or twice.

2. Line a baking sheet with waxed paper. Drop chocolate mixture in 1-inch mounds onto prepared baking sheet. Chill about 1 hour or until firm. Shape chilled mounds into 1-inch balls; return to baking sheet. Cover and freeze for 30 minutes.

3. Place white chocolate and shortening in a large microwave-safe bowl. Microwave, uncovered, on 50 percent power (medium) for 2 to 2½ minutes or until melted, stirring twice. Cool slightly. Dip balls, one at a time, into melted chocolate. Let excess chocolate drip off balls. Place truffles on a baking sheet lined with waxed paper. Immediately sprinkle each truffle with some of the coffee crystals. Chill about 30 minutes or until set.

4. Cover tightly and chill for up to 2 weeks or freeze for up to 1 month. Let truffles stand at room temperature about 30 minutes before serving.

Per truffle: 116 cal., 8 g total fat (3 g sat. fat), 8 mg chol., 15 mg sodium, 10 g carbo., 1 g fiber, 1 g pro.

Mocha
Truffles

Pumpkin Fudge

Pumpkin Fudge

Set out squares of this pumpkin confection alongside chocolate fudge for a mouthwatering display.

Prep: 10 minutes **Cook:** 20 minutes **Cool:** 2 hours
Makes: about 96 pieces

3	cups sugar
¾	cup butter
1	5-ounce can evaporated milk
½	cup canned pumpkin
1	10-ounce package cinnamon-flavor pieces
1	7-ounce jar marshmallow creme
¾	cup chopped walnuts, toasted (see Note, page 17)

1. Line a 13×9×2-inch baking pan with foil, extending foil over edges of pan. Butter foil; set pan aside.

2. In a 3-quart heavy saucepan combine sugar, butter, evaporated milk, and pumpkin. Cook and stir over medium-high heat until mixture boils. Clip a candy thermometer to side of pan. Reduce heat to medium-low; continue boiling at a moderate, steady rate, stirring frequently, until thermometer registers 234°F, soft-ball stage (20 to 25 minutes). (Adjust heat as necessary to maintain a steady boil.)

3. Remove saucepan from heat; remove thermometer from saucepan. Stir in cinnamon-flavor pieces until melted. Stir in marshmallow creme and walnuts.

4. Immediately spread fudge evenly in prepared pan. Score into squares while warm. Let fudge cool to room temperature. When fudge is firm, use foil to lift it out of pan. Cut into squares. Cover tightly and chill for up to 1 week. Do not freeze.

Per piece: 68 cal., 3 g total fat (2 g sat. fat), 4 mg chol., 14 mg sodium, 10 g carbo., 0 g fiber, 0 g pro.

Easy Espresso Fudge

A luscious infusion of espresso wakes up this rich, creamy chocolate fudge.

Prep: 20 minutes **Chill:** 2 hours **Makes:** 64 pieces

	Nonstick cooking spray
3	cups semisweet chocolate pieces
1	14-ounce can sweetened condensed milk
2	tablespoons instant espresso powder or instant coffee crystals
1	cup hazelnuts (filberts) or almonds, chopped and toasted (see Note, page 17)
1	teaspoon vanilla

1. Line an 8×8×2-inch baking pan with foil, extending foil over edges of pan. Lightly coat foil with nonstick cooking spray; set aside.

2. In a 2-quart heavy saucepan cook and stir chocolate pieces, sweetened condensed milk, and espresso powder over low heat just until chocolate melts and mixture is smooth. Remove saucepan from heat; stir in nuts and vanilla. Spread evenly in prepared pan. Cover and chill about 2 hours or until firm.

3. Use foil to lift fudge out of pan. Cut into 1-inch squares. Cover tightly and chill for up to 1 week or freeze for up to 3 months. Let fudge stand at room temperature about 30 minutes before serving.

Per piece: 73 cal., 4 g total fat (2 g sat. fat), 2 mg chol., 9 mg sodium, 9 g carbo., 1 g fiber, 1 g pro.

Creamy Chocolate Rum Fudge

Rum, rum, rum … the buttery, fragrant liquor has its way with this creamy, nutty fudge.

Prep: 20 minutes **Cook:** 10 minutes **Cool:** 55 minutes
Makes: about 1 pound (about 30 pieces)

2	cups sugar
¾	cup half-and-half or light cream
2	ounces sweet baking chocolate, chopped
1	teaspoon light-color corn syrup
2	tablespoons butter
1	teaspoon vanilla
¼	teaspoon rum flavoring
½	cup chopped pecans, toasted (see Note, page 17) (optional)

1. Line a 9×5×3-inch loaf pan with foil, extending foil over edges of pan. Butter foil; set pan aside.

2. Butter the sides of a 2-quart heavy saucepan. In saucepan combine sugar, half-and-half, chocolate, corn syrup, and ⅛ teaspoon *salt*. Cook and stir over medium-high heat until mixture boils. Clip a candy thermometer to side of pan. Reduce heat to medium-low; continue boiling at a moderate, steady rate, stirring occasionally, until thermometer registers 236°F, soft-ball stage (10 to 15 minutes). (Adjust heat to maintain a steady boil.)

3. Remove saucepan from heat. Add butter, vanilla, and rum flavoring, but do not stir. Cool, without stirring, about 55 minutes or until thermometer registers 110°F.

4. Remove thermometer from saucepan. If desired, stir in pecans. Beat vigorously with a wooden spoon about 5 minutes or until the fudge becomes very thick and just starts to lose its gloss.

5. Immediately spread fudge evenly in prepared pan. Score into squares while warm. Let fudge cool to room temperature. When fudge is firm, use foil to lift it out of pan. Cut into squares.

6. Cover tightly and chill for up to 1 week or freeze for up to 3 months. Let fudge stand at room temperature about 30 minutes before serving.

Per piece: 76 cal., 2 g total fat (1 g sat. fat), 4 mg chol., 18 mg sodium, 15 g carbo., 0 g fiber, 0 g pro.

Candy-Box Caramels

Dress up purchased caramels with candy coating, finely chopped nuts, and nonpareils.

Prep: 40 minutes Stand: 1 hour Makes: 48 pieces

- 12 ounces chocolate- and/or vanilla-flavor candy coating, coarsely chopped
- 1 cup toffee pieces, crushed; finely chopped pistachio nuts; and/or nonpareils
- 48 short plastic or wooden skewers (optional)
- 1 14-ounce package (about 48) vanilla caramels, unwrapped
- 2 ounces chocolate- and/or vanilla-flavor candy coating, coarsely chopped (optional)

1. In a microwave-safe 4-cup measuring cup, place the 12 ounces candy coating. Microwave on 100 percent power (high) about 3 minutes or until melted, stirring every 30 seconds.

2. Place toffee pieces in a shallow dish. If desired, insert a skewer into each caramel. Dip one caramel into melted candy coating; turn to coat as much of the caramel as desired, allowing excess coating to drip off caramel. (If not using skewers, use a fork to lift caramel out of candy coating, drawing the fork across the measuring cup rim to remove excess coating from caramel.) Place dipped caramel in toffee pieces, turning to coat. Place coated caramel on a baking sheet lined with waxed paper. Repeat with remaining caramels. Let caramels stand about 1 hour or until coating dries.

3. If desired, place 2 ounces of a contrasting color of candy coating in a microwave-safe bowl. Microwave, uncovered, on 100 percent power (high) about 2 minutes or until melted, stirring every 30 seconds. Cool slightly. Transfer coating to a small, heavy plastic bag. Cut a small hole in one corner of bag and drizzle coating over coated caramels. Let caramels stand until set.

4. Store tightly covered at room temperature for up to 1 week or freeze for up to 3 months.

Per piece: 91 cal., 4 g total fat (3 g sat. fat), 2 mg chol., 31 mg sodium, 13 g carbo., 0 g fiber, 1 g pro.

Candy-Box Caramels

cookie exchange

For many, cookies are the
creative medium of the season.
How can we shape, flavor,
roll, cut, or decorate them?
The renditions are countless.
Whether packed on a covered
plate for neighbors, in a tin
arriving from family, or with
milk before bed, cookies win
our hearts, melt our restraint,
and make our mouths water.

Tender Sugar Cookies,
page 118

Cran-Crazy Cookies

Prep: 30 minutes **Bake:** 10 minutes per batch
Oven: 350°F **Makes:** about 60 cookies

- ¾ **cup butter, softened**
- 1½ **cups packed brown sugar**
- 2 **teaspoons finely shredded lemon peel**
- ½ **teaspoon baking soda**
- ½ **teaspoon baking powder**
- ¼ **teaspoon salt**
- 2 **eggs**
- 2 **teaspoons vanilla**
- 2⅓ **cups whole wheat flour**
- 1½ **cups chopped walnuts, toasted
  (see Note, page 17)**
- 1½ **cups dried cranberries**

**Cran-Crazy
Cookies**

**Honey-Nut
Oatmeal Drops**

1. Preheat oven to 350°F. In a large mixing bowl
beat butter with an electric mixer on medium to
high speed for 30 seconds. Add brown sugar,
lemon peel, baking soda, baking powder, and salt.
Beat until combined, scraping sides of bowl
occasionally. Beat in eggs and vanilla. Beat in as
much of the flour as you can with the mixer. Stir in
any remaining flour. Stir in walnuts and cranberries.

2. Drop dough by rounded teaspoons 2 inches
apart onto ungreased cookie sheets. Bake for 10 to
12 minutes or until edges are light brown. Cool on
cookie sheets for 2 minutes. Transfer to wire racks
and let cool.

Per cookie: 88 cal., 5 g total fat (2 g sat. fat), 13 mg chol.,
43 mg sodium, 12 g carbo., 1 g fiber, 1 g pro.

Honey-Nut Oatmeal Drops

*A sprinkling of sugar before baking gives these cookies
a sweet sparkle. A touch of honey makes them soft
and chewy.*

Prep: 25 minutes **Bake:** 8 minutes per batch
Oven: 350°F **Makes:** about 60 cookies

- 1 **cup butter, softened**
- 1 **cup packed brown sugar**
- 1 **teaspoon baking soda**
- ½ **teaspoon salt**
- ½ **cup honey**
- 2 **eggs**
- 2 **teaspoons vanilla**
- 2¼ **cups all-purpose flour**
- 2½ **cups quick-cooking rolled oats**
- ¾ **cup chopped honey-roasted peanuts
  Granulated sugar**

1. Preheat oven to 350°F. Line a cookie sheet with
parchment paper; set aside. In a large mixing bowl
beat butter with an electric mixer on medium to
high speed for 30 seconds. Add brown sugar,

baking soda, and salt. Beat until combined, scraping sides of bowl occasionally. Beat in honey, eggs, and vanilla. Beat in as much of the flour as you can with the mixer. Stir in any remaining flour. Stir in oats and peanuts.

2. Drop dough by rounded teaspoons 2 inches apart onto prepared cookie sheet. Lightly sprinkle tops of dough mounds with granulated sugar. Bake for 8 to 10 minutes or until golden brown. Cool on cookie sheet for 2 minutes. Transfer to a wire rack and let cool.

Per cookie: 91 cal., 4 g total fat (2 g sat. fat), 15 mg chol., 70 mg sodium, 13 g carbo., 1 g fiber, 1 g pro.

White Chocolate-Cherry Shortbread

A dip in melted white chocolate and a roll in nonpareils and edible glitter give color and texture to these cookies.

Prep: 40 minutes **Bake:** 10 minutes per batch
Oven: 325°F **Makes:** about 60 cookies

½	cup maraschino cherries, drained and finely chopped
2½	cups all-purpose flour
½	cup sugar
1	cup butter
12	ounces white baking chocolate with cocoa butter, finely chopped
½	teaspoon almond extract
2	drops red food coloring (optional)
2	teaspoons shortening
	White nonpareils and/or red edible glitter (optional)

1. Preheat oven to 325°F. Spread chopped cherries on paper towels to drain well.

2. In a large bowl combine flour and sugar. Using a pastry blender, cut in butter until mixture resembles fine crumbs. Stir in drained cherries and 4 ounces (⅔ cup) of the chopped white chocolate. Stir in almond extract and, if desired, food coloring. Knead mixture until it forms a smooth ball.

3. Shape dough into ¾-inch balls. Place balls 2 inches apart on an ungreased cookie sheet. Using the bottom of a drinking glass dipped in sugar, flatten balls to 1½-inch rounds.

4. Bake for 10 to 12 minutes or until centers are set. Cool on cookie sheet for 1 minute. Transfer to a wire rack and let cool.

5. In a small saucepan combine the remaining 8 ounces white chocolate and the shortening. Cook and stir over low heat until melted and smooth. Dip half of each cookie into the melted chocolate, allowing excess to drip off. If desired, roll dipped edge in nonpareils and/or edible glitter. Let cookies stand until chocolate sets.

Per cookie: 88 cal., 5 g total fat (3 g sat. fat), 9 mg chol., 28 mg sodium, 9 g carbo., 0 g fiber, 1 g pro.

White Chocolate-Cherry Shortbread

Pumpkin-Spiced Star
Cookie Cutouts

combined. Beat in as much of the flour as you can with the mixer. Stir in any remaining flour. If necessary, cover and chill dough for 30 to 60 minutes or until easy to handle.

2. Preheat oven to 300°F. Shape dough into 1-inch balls. Roll balls in the remaining ¼ cup sugar.* Place balls 2 inches apart on ungreased cookie sheets. Bake about 15 minutes or until tops are slightly cracked and sides are set (do not let edges brown). Transfer to wire racks and let cool.

*Tip: For a colorful platter of cookies, roll the dough balls in different colored sugars instead of the white granulated sugar.

Per cookie: 62 cal., 3 g total fat (2 g sat. fat), 12 mg chol., 39 mg sodium, 8 g carbo., 0 g fiber, 1 g pro.

Pumpkin-Spiced Star Cookie Cutouts

Brown Butter Icing, the luscious, caramelized frosting so popular in the '50s, makes a stellar comeback on top of these spicy cookies.

Prep: 30 minutes **Bake:** 8 minutes per batch
Oven: 375°F
Makes: 36 large cookies or 72 small cookies

  1   **17.5-ounce package sugar cookie mix**
  ⅓   **cup butter, melted**
  1   **egg**
  2   **teaspoons pumpkin pie spice**
  ½   **teaspoon ground nutmeg**
  1   **recipe Brown Butter Icing**

1. Preheat oven to 375°F. In a large bowl combine dry cookie mix, butter, egg, pumpkin pie spice, and nutmeg. Stir with a wooden spoon until a stiff dough forms (if necessary, knead dough to combine).

2. On a lightly floured surface, roll dough until ¼ inch thick. Using a 1½- to 2½-inch star-shape cookie cutter, cut out dough. Place 1 inch apart on an ungreased cookie sheet.

3. Bake about 8 minutes or until bottoms are light brown. Cool on cookie sheet for 1 minute. Transfer to a wire rack and let cool. Drizzle with Brown Butter Icing.

Tender Sugar Cookies

These cookies bake longer and at a lower temperature than most cookies. To retain tenderness, don't let them brown. See photo, page 115.

Prep: 40 minutes **Bake:** 15 minutes per batch
Chill: 30 minutes **Oven:** 300°F
Makes: about 60 cookies

  1   **cup butter, softened**
1¼   **cups sugar**
  1   **teaspoon baking powder**
  ¼   **teaspoon salt**
  1   **egg**
  1   **teaspoon vanilla**
2¼   **cups all-purpose flour**

1. In a large mixing bowl beat butter with an electric mixer on medium to high speed for 30 seconds. Add 1 cup of the sugar, baking powder, and salt. Beat until combined, scraping sides of bowl occasionally. Beat in egg and vanilla until

Brown Butter Icing: In a small saucepan heat 2 tablespoons butter over low heat about 15 minutes or until brown (be careful not to burn). Remove saucepan from heat. Stir in 2 cups powdered sugar, 2 tablespoons milk, and 1 teaspoon vanilla. Immediately drizzle over cooled cookies (icing will harden quickly).

Per large cookie: 109 cal., 4 g total fat (2 g sat. fat), 12 mg chol., 51 mg sodium, 18 g carbo., 0 g fiber, 1 g pro.

Cranberry-Eggnog Twirls

Nutmeg and rum extract give these cookies an intense flavor of rich, creamy eggnog. Cranberries provide tangy flavor.

Prep: 25 minutes Bake: 10 minutes per batch
Chill: 5 hours Oven: 375°F
Makes: about 60 cookies

1	cup butter, softened
1½	cups sugar
½	teaspoon baking powder
½	teaspoon salt
½	teaspoon ground nutmeg
2	eggs
1	teaspoon rum extract
3¼	cups all-purpose flour
½	cup cranberry preserves or jam
1½	teaspoons cornstarch
½	cup finely chopped pecans, toasted (see Note, page 17)

1. In a large bowl beat butter with an electric mixer on medium to high speed for 30 seconds. Add sugar, baking powder, salt, and nutmeg. Beat until combined, scraping bowl occasionally. Beat in eggs and rum extract until combined. Beat in as much of the flour as you can with the mixer. Stir in any remaining flour. Divide dough in half. Cover and chill dough about 1 hour or until easy to handle.

2. Meanwhile, for filling, in a small saucepan combine preserves and cornstarch. Cook and stir until thickened and bubbly. Remove saucepan from heat; stir in pecans. Cover and set aside to cool.

3. Roll half of the dough between two pieces of waxed paper into a 10-inch square. Spread half of the filling over dough square to within ½ inch

of edges; roll up dough. Moisten edges; pinch to seal. Wrap in waxed paper or plastic wrap. Repeat with remaining dough and filling. Chill for 4 to 24 hours.

4. Preheat oven to 375°F. Line large cookie sheets with parchment paper. Cut rolls into ¼-inch slices. Place slices 2 inches apart on prepared cookie sheets.

5. Bake for 10 to 12 minutes or until edges are firm and bottoms are light brown. Cool on cookie sheets for 1 minute. Transfer to a wire rack and let cool.

Per cookie: 88 cal., 4 g total fat (2 g sat. fat), 15 mg chol., 48 mg sodium, 12 g carbo., 0 g fiber, 1 g pro.

Cranberry-Eggnog Twirls

Peppermint-Twist Biscotti

Prep: 30 minutes **Bake:** 40 minutes **Cool:** 1 hour
Oven: 375°F/300°F **Makes:** about 72 cookies

- ⅔ cup butter, softened
- 1⅓ cups sugar
- 1 tablespoon baking powder
- ¼ teaspoon salt
- 4 eggs
- ½ teaspoon peppermint extract
- 4¼ cups all-purpose flour
- 1 cup coarsely chopped candy canes
  Red paste food coloring
- 1 recipe Peppermint Icing
  Chopped candy canes (optional)

1. Preheat oven to 375°F. Line cookie sheet with foil; set aside. In a large mixing bowl beat butter with an electric mixer on medium to high speed for 30 seconds. Add sugar, baking powder, and salt. Beat until combined, scraping sides of bowl occasionally. Beat in eggs and peppermint extract. Beat in as much of the flour as you can with the mixer. Stir in any remaining flour. Stir in the 1 cup chopped candy canes.

2. Divide dough in half; tint one portion of dough with food coloring. Divide each dough half into three portions. On a lightly floured surface, roll each dough portion into a 14-inch-long rope.

3. On prepared cookie sheet, place one rope of each color side by side. Twist ropes around each other several times; flatten slightly until about 2 inches wide. Repeat with remaining ropes, placing twists about 4 inches apart on cookie sheet.

4. Bake for 20 to 25 minutes or until light brown and tops are cracked. Cool on cookie sheet for 1 hour. Carefully peel away foil.

5. Preheat oven to 300°F. Transfer twists to a cutting board. Use a serrated knife to cut each twist diagonally into ½-inch slices. Place slices on an ungreased cookie sheet. Bake for 10 minutes. Turn slices over; bake for 10 to 15 minutes more or until crisp and dry. Transfer to a wire rack and let cool.

6. Drizzle cookies with Peppermint Icing. If desired, sprinkle with additional chopped candy canes. Let cookies stand until icing sets.

Peppermint Icing: In a medium bowl combine 2 cups powdered sugar and 1 tablespoon peppermint schnapps (or use 1 tablespoon milk and ¼ teaspoon peppermint extract); stir until smooth. Add enough additional peppermint schnapps or milk (about 2 tablespoons) to make icing drizzling consistency.

Per cookie: 82 cal., 2 g total fat (1 g sat. fat), 16 mg chol., 35 mg sodium, 14 g carbo., 0 g fiber, 1 g pro.

Yummy No-Bake Bars

Prep: 25 minutes **Chill:** 1 hour **Makes:** 64 bars

- 1 cup granulated sugar
- 1 cup light-color corn syrup
- 2 cups peanut butter
- 3 cups crisp rice cereal
- 3 cups cornflakes
- ¾ cup butter
- 4 cups powdered sugar
- 2 4-serving-size packages vanilla instant pudding and pie filling mix
- ¼ cup milk
- 1 12-ounce package semisweet chocolate pieces
- ½ cup butter

1. Line a 15×10×1-inch baking pan with foil, extending foil over edges of pan; set pan aside.

2. In a large saucepan combine granulated sugar and corn syrup. Heat and stir just until mixture boils around edges. Heat and stir for 1 minute more. Remove saucepan from heat. Stir in peanut

Peppermint-
Twist Biscotti

Yummy
No-Bake Bars

butter until melted. Stir in rice cereal and cornflakes until coated. Press mixture into the bottom of prepared pan.

3. For pudding layer, in a medium saucepan melt the ¾ cup butter. Stir in powdered sugar, dry vanilla pudding mixes, and milk. Spread pudding mixture evenly over cereal layer; set aside.

4. For frosting, in a small saucepan combine chocolate pieces and the ½ cup butter. Heat and stir over low heat until melted and smooth. Spread frosting over pudding layer. Cover and chill about 1 hour or until set. To serve, use foil to lift out of pan. Cut into bars.

Per bar: 182 cal., 9 g total fat (4 g sat. fat), 10 mg chol., 133 mg sodium, 25 g carbo., 1 g fiber, 2 g pro.

Cookie Exchange

This idea for baking one kind of cookie and trading with friends to create an assortment is more popular than ever.

A cookie swap works well with a group of neighbors, members of an organization, or coworkers. Or simply gather some friends and relatives for a holiday party.

Pick a date early and send, phone, or e-mail invitations. Unless the exchange will be part of a group's regular meeting, it's important to get your date on guests' calendars as soon as possible.

Let guests know the rules
Ask guests to bring one kind of special homemade holiday cookie (no store-bought sweets allowed).

Specify the number of cookies each person must bring: three to four dozen is probably the minimum to ensure that each guest takes home a good sampling.

Suggest that everyone bring extra plastic bags or cartons so each type of cookie has its own container for the trip home. That way they're ready to pop into the freezer to enjoy later. Or bring the cookies to the party already divided and plated or bagged.

Let guests know if they should provide copies of their recipes or will be expected to share the origins or some other story about the recipes.

What to serve
Can't resist sampling the cookies at the party? Then have guests bring a separate plate for a tasting buffet. Otherwise there may not be enough cookies left to exchange.

Depending on the time of day, consider serving brunch or a salad lunch. Or have a salad potluck supper. If the party is at your workplace, plan for each guest to bring a sandwich while the hosts provide a holiday beverage and fruit or dessert.

More exchange ideas
Turn your cookie exchange into a fundraiser for a favorite charity. Ask guests to bring a gift for a sponsored family, a local food pantry, or a holiday hat-and-mitten tree.

Combine holiday activities, such as tree trimming or caroling, or winter sports, such as sledding, ice-skating, or cross-country skiing, with a family cookie exchange.

Stick with a theme. Host an all-chocolate or nice-and-spicy exchange. Or assign each guest a country or region, requesting them to learn a holiday tradition or to make a cookie from the assigned country to share.

time
for tea

Whether your tea party is spontaneous, planned, or just you and yours enjoying rare moments together, these sweet and savory goodies along with fragrant teas will help you mark the occasion.

Cucumber Canapés,
page 129

Pomegranate Tea

Pomegranate juice provides a colorful flavor twist to brewed tea.

Start to Finish: 40 minutes
Makes: four (8-ounce) servings

- 3 cups water
- 3 tablespoons sugar
- 1 family-size tea bag or 4 regular-size tea bags
- 1 cup pomegranate juice
- ¼ teaspoon almond extract
  Lemon wedges (optional)

1. In a medium saucepan bring water and sugar to boiling; remove from heat. Add tea bag; let stand, covered, for 30 minutes. Discard tea bag. Stir in pomegranate juice and almond extract. Serve hot or iced with lemon wedges.

Per serving: 75 cal., 0 g total fat (0 g sat. fat), 0 mg chol., 8 mg sodium, 19 g carbo., 0 g fiber, 0 g pro.

Mulled Holiday Tea

This wine-laced tea provides guests with a spirited beverage option. However, for the traditionalists and teetotalers on your guest list, also offer a good, strong black tea, such as English breakfast tea, alongside cream and sugar.

Start to Finish: 25 minutes
Makes: about twelve (6-ounce) servings

- 7 bags black tea (such as Darjeeling)
- 4 cups boiling water
- 4 cups apple juice

- 2 cups dry red wine
- ½ cup packed brown sugar
- 1 3-inch piece stick cinnamon
- 1 teaspoon whole cloves
- ¼ teaspoon cardamom seeds

1. Place tea bags in a 4-quart Dutch oven. Pour the boiling water over tea bags; let stand for 5 minutes. Discard tea bags. Stir in apple juice, wine, and brown sugar.

2. For spice bag, place cinnamon, cloves, and cardamom in the center of a double-thick, 6-inch square of 100-percent-cotton cheesecloth. Bring corners together and tie with a clean kitchen string. Add spice bag to Dutch oven. Bring just to boiling; reduce heat. Simmer, covered, for 10 minutes. Discard spice bag.

Per serving: 108 cal., 0 g total fat (0 g sat. fat), 0 mg chol., 9 mg sodium, 20 g carbo., 0 g fiber, 0 g pro.

Cranberry-Apple Strudel Rolls

Phyllo dough is actually relatively easy to work with, but it does dry quickly once unwrapped. When using, keep the stack of dough covered with plastic wrap and remove sheets only as needed. Sheet size varies with manufacturer, but the 14×9-inch rectangles called for here are the most common.

Prep: 35 minutes **Bake:** 15 minutes **Oven:** 375°F
Makes: 24 rolls

- 1 cup cranberries
- ⅓ cup water
- ⅔ cup chopped apple
- ¼ cup golden raisins
- ⅓ cup granulated sugar
- ½ teaspoon finely shredded orange peel
- ½ teaspoon ground cinnamon
- 12 sheets frozen phyllo dough
  (14×9-inch rectangles), thawed
- ½ cup butter, melted
- ⅓ cup very finely chopped walnuts
  Powdered sugar

1. In a small saucepan combine cranberries and water. Bring to boiling; reduce heat. Simmer, uncovered, about 3 minutes or until cranberries pop. Drain cranberries; discard liquid.

Pomegranate Tea

2. In another saucepan stir together cranberries, apple, and raisins; add granulated sugar, orange peel, and cinnamon; toss gently to combine. Set aside.

3. Preheat oven to 375°F. Unfold phyllo dough. Layer 3 sheets of phyllo on a cutting board or flat surface, brushing each sheet lightly with some of the melted butter and sprinkling lightly with some of the walnuts. (Keep phyllo dough covered with plastic wrap to prevent it from drying out; remove sheets as needed.) Cut phyllo stack crosswise into thirds, then lengthwise in half to form six almost square pieces. Repeat with the remaining phyllo sheets, more of the melted butter, and the remaining walnuts.

4. Spoon a scant tablespoon of the fruit mixture in a thin strip near the bottom edge of each phyllo piece. Fold bottom edge of phyllo up and over fruit mixture. Roll up to enclose fruit mixture, folding in sides as you roll.

5. Place rolls, seam sides down, on a foil-lined baking sheet. Brush with remaining melted butter. Bake for 15 to 18 minutes or until golden brown. Transfer to a wire rack and let cool. Just before serving, sprinkle with powdered sugar.

Per roll: 94 cal., 5 g total fat (3 g sat. fat), 10 mg chol., 74 mg sodium, 11 g carbo., 1 g fiber, 1 g pro.

Coconut Cupcakes

Each dainty cupcake is topped with a generous amount of fluffy frosting and coconut.

Prep: 20 minutes **Bake:** 12 minutes **Oven:** 350°F
Makes: 24 cupcakes

- ⅔ cup all-purpose flour
- ½ teaspoon baking powder
- ⅛ teaspoon baking soda
  Dash salt
- ¼ cup butter, softened
- ½ cup sugar
- ½ teaspoon vanilla
- 1 egg
- ¼ cup buttermilk
- 1 recipe Creamy Frosting
- 1 cup flaked coconut

Coconut Cupcakes

1. Preheat oven to 350°F. Grease and lightly flour twenty-four 1¾-inch muffin cups or line with paper bake cups; set aside. In a bowl combine flour, baking powder, baking soda, and salt; set aside.

2. In a medium mixing bowl beat butter with an electric mixer on medium to high speed about 30 seconds. Add sugar and vanilla. Beat about 2 minutes or until light and fluffy, scraping sides of bowl. Add egg; beat until combined. Alternately add the flour mixture and buttermilk to the egg mixture, beating on low to medium speed after each addition just until combined.

3. Spoon about 1 rounded measuring teaspoon of the batter into each prepared muffin cup. Bake about 12 minutes or until a wooden toothpick inserted in the centers comes out clean. Cool in muffin cups on a wire rack for 5 minutes. Remove from muffin cups; cool completely on a wire rack.

4. Spread Creamy Frosting over each cupcake; sprinkle with coconut. Serve immediately or cover and chill for up to 4 hours.

Creamy Frosting: In a large mixing bowl beat together 4 ounces softened cream cheese and 2 tablespoons softened butter with an electric mixer on medium to high speed until combined. Beat in 1 teaspoon vanilla. Gradually add 2½ cups powdered sugar, beating until smooth.

Per cupcake: 148 cal., 6 g total fat (4 g sat. fat), 22 mg chol., 74 mg sodium, 22 g carbo., 0 g fiber, 1 g pro.

Little Lemon Tarts

Old-fashioned lemon curd lends a Victorian touch to these tarts. Today the lemon curd and cookie dough can be purchased for 21st-century convenience.

Prep: 25 minutes **Bake:** 10 minutes **Oven:** 350°F
Makes: 24 tarts

  Nonstick cooking spray
1 18-ounce roll refrigerated sugar cookie dough
2 10-ounce jars (1½ cups) lemon curd

1. Preheat oven to 350°F. Lightly coat twenty-four 2½-inch muffin cups with cooking spray; set aside. Cut cookie dough into 12 slices; cut each slice in half. Press each piece of cookie dough evenly into the bottom and halfway up the sides of the prepared muffin cups.

2. Bake for 10 to 12 minutes or until edges are light brown and set. Cool in pans for 5 minutes. Loosen edges; cool 5 minutes more. Carefully remove tart shells from pans. Cool completely on wire racks.

3. Just before serving, spoon about 1 tablespoon of the lemon curd into each tart shell. If desired, top with *kumquat slices, pomegranate seeds,* and *mint sprigs.*

Make-Ahead Directions: Prepare as directed through Step 2. Place tart shells in an airtight container. Store at room temperature for up to 3 days or freeze for up to 1 month. Thaw frozen tart shells in container at room temperature for 1 hour before filling with lemon curd.

Per tart: 170 cal., 6 g total fat (2 g sat. fat), 24 mg chol., 108 mg sodium, 30 g carbo., 3 g fiber, 1 g pro.

Toffee-Almond Shortbread

You will love the something extra that toffee, almonds, and a drizzle of chocolate add.

Prep: 20 minutes **Bake:** 16 minutes **Oven:** 325°F
Makes: 16 cookies

1¼ cups all-purpose flour
3 tablespoons packed brown sugar
½ cup butter

2 tablespoons finely chopped almonds, toasted (see Note, page 17)
¼ cup toffee pieces, slightly crushed
2 ounces semisweet chocolate, melted

1. Preheat oven to 325°F. In a medium bowl combine flour and brown sugar. Using a pastry blender, cut in butter until mixture resembles fine crumbs and starts to cling. Stir in almonds and 2 tablespoons of the toffee pieces. Form the mixture into a ball and knead until smooth.

2. On a lightly floured surface, roll dough into an 8½-inch square. Trim edges to form an 8-inch square; discard scraps. Cut dough into 16 squares. Place 1 inch apart on an ungreased cookie sheet. Bake for 16 to 18 minutes or until bottoms just start to brown. Transfer to a wire rack and let cool.

3. Drizzle some of the melted chocolate over 8 of the cookies. Dip one end of each of the remaining 8 cookies into the remaining melted chocolate; dip into the remaining toffee pieces. Let stand until set.

Per cookie: 135 cal., 8 g total fat (5 g sat. fat), 18 mg chol., 57 mg sodium, 13 g carbo., 1 g fiber, 1 g pro.

Raspberry-Crowned Orange Brownies

Replete with refined touches such as bittersweet chocolate and orange liqueur, easy-to-make brownies become a sophisticated choice with tea.

Prep: 30 minutes **Bake:** 20 minutes **Oven:** 350°F
Cool: 30 minutes **Makes:** 24 brownies

½ cup butter
2 ounces unsweetened chocolate, chopped
2 eggs
¾ cup sugar
⅓ cup orange marmalade
2 teaspoons orange liqueur
¾ cup all-purpose flour
½ teaspoon baking powder
1 recipe Chocolate-Orange Frosting
2 ounces bittersweet or semisweet chocolate, chopped
1 teaspoon shortening
1 pint fresh raspberries
  Unsweetened cocoa powder (optional)

Little Lemon Tarts, Raspberry-Crowned Orange Brownies, and Toffee-Almond Shortbread

1. Preheat oven to 350°F. Line an 8×8×2-inch baking pan with foil, extending foil over edges of pan. Lightly grease foil; set pan aside.

2. In a medium saucepan melt butter and the unsweetened chocolate over low heat, stirring occasionally. Remove saucepan from heat; cool about 5 minutes. Stir in eggs, sugar, orange marmalade, and orange liqueur. Stir in flour and baking powder. Spread batter into prepared pan.

3. Bake for 20 to 25 minutes or until top springs back when lightly touched. Cool on a wire rack for 30 minutes. Use foil to lift brownies out of pan.

4. Pour Chocolate-Orange Frosting over brownies, spreading evenly. Let stand until set. Use a long, sharp knife to cut brownies into 24 rectangles. Before serving, in a small heavy saucepan melt the bittersweet chocolate and shortening over low heat, stirring constantly; cool slightly. Place chocolate

mixture in a heavy resealable plastic bag. Cut a small hole in one corner of the bag; drizzle chocolate mixture in a zigzag pattern over each brownie. Top each with raspberries. If desired, sift cocoa powder over each brownie. Let stand until chocolate sets.

Chocolate-Orange Frosting: In a small saucepan melt 2 ounces bittersweet or semisweet chocolate, chopped, and 2 tablespoons butter over low heat, stirring occasionally; remove from heat. Stir in ¾ cup powdered sugar, 4 teaspoons hot water, and 1 teaspoon finely shredded orange peel until combined.

Per brownie: 153 cal., 8 g total fat (5 g sat. fat), 30 mg chol., 48 mg sodium, 20 g carbo., 1 g fiber, 2 g pro.

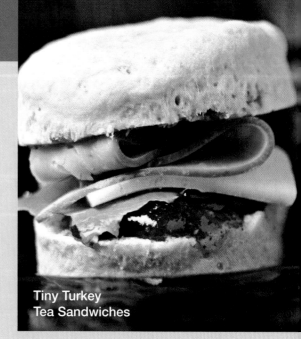

**Tiny Turkey
Tea Sandwiches**

Cheese Tartlets

*Look for baked miniature phyllo dough shells
in the frozen food section or the baking aisle
of your supermarket.*

Prep: 25 minutes **Bake:** 10 minutes **Oven:** 350°F
Makes: 30 tartlets

- ¼ cup finely chopped onion
- 1 clove garlic, minced
- 2 teaspoons olive oil
- 4 ounces soft goat cheese (chèvre)
- 1 egg, lightly beaten
- ½ cup freshly grated Parmesan cheese
- ¼ teaspoon freshly ground black pepper
  Dash salt
- 3 tablespoons snipped fresh basil
- 2 2.1-ounce packages (30) baked miniature
  phyllo dough shells

1. In a small skillet cook onion and garlic in hot
oil over medium heat until tender.

2. Preheat oven to 350°F. In a medium bowl stir
goat cheese to soften; stir in egg until combined.
Stir in Parmesan cheese, pepper, and salt. Stir in
onion mixture and basil.

3. Arrange phyllo shells in a shallow baking pan.
Fill each shell with 1 rounded teaspoon of the
cheese mixture. Bake for 10 to 12 minutes or until
filling is set. Serve warm.

Per tartlet: 47 cal., 3 g total fat (1 g sat. fat), 10 mg chol.,
63 mg sodium, 3 g carbo., 0 g fiber, 2 g pro.

Tiny Turkey Tea Sandwiches

Prep: 35 minutes **Bake:** 12 minutes **Oven:** 425°F
Makes: 24 to 30 sandwiches

- 1 recipe Tiny Sweet Potato Biscuits
- ⅔ cup fruit chutney, snipped
- 1 cup fresh baby spinach leaves, arugula,
  or mesclun, stems trimmed
- 3 ounces thinly sliced Havarti or Muenster
  cheese, cut to fit biscuits
- 6 ounces thinly sliced smoked turkey,
  cut and folded to fit biscuits

1. Use a fork to split the cooled Tiny Sweet Potato
Biscuits in half. Spread about ½ teaspoon chutney
on the cut side of each biscuit bottom. Top each
with 1 or 2 spinach leaves, some cheese, and some
turkey. Spread the cut side of each biscuit top with
½ teaspoon chutney; place on top of turkey.

Tiny Sweet Potato Biscuits: Preheat oven to
425°F. In a large bowl stir together 1½ cups
all-purpose flour, 1 tablespoon sugar, 1 teaspoon
baking powder, ½ teaspoon baking soda, and
½ teaspoon salt. Using a pastry blender, cut in
¼ cup cold butter until mixture resembles coarse
crumbs. Make a well in the center of the flour
mixture. In a small bowl stir together ½ cup
buttermilk and ½ cup mashed cooked sweet potato.
Add sweet potato mixture to flour mixture, stirring
just until combined. Turn dough out onto a well-
floured surface. Knead dough by folding and gently
pressing for 10 to 12 strokes. Lightly roll or pat
dough until ½ inch thick. Using a floured 1½-inch
to 2-inch biscuit cutter, cut dough into circles.
Reroll scraps as necessary and dip cutter into flour
between cuts. Place biscuits 1 inch apart on a large
ungreased baking sheet. Bake for 12 to 14 minutes
or until light brown. Immediately remove biscuits
from baking sheet. Cool on a wire rack. Makes
24 to 30 biscuits.

Make-Ahead Directions: Prepare and bake
Tiny Sweet Potato Biscuits; cool completely.
Place biscuits in a freezer container; freeze for
up to 3 months. Thaw at room temperature.

Per sandwich: 90 cal., 4 g total fat (1 g sat. fat), 15 mg chol.,
216 mg sodium, 10 g carbo., 1 g fiber, 4 g pro.

Garden-Style Puff Pastry Sandwiches

Make party sandwiches by stuffing split puff pastry with cheese and vegetables.

Prep: 45 minutes **Bake:** 10 minutes **Oven:** 375°F
Makes: 32 sandwiches

1⅓ cups soft herbed goat cheese (chèvre) or
     two 5-ounce containers semisoft cheese
     with garlic and herbs
  2 tablespoons finely chopped green onion
  6 to 8 teaspoons hot-style prepared
     horseradish
  1 17.3-ounce package frozen puff pastry
     (2 sheets), thawed
  1 tablespoon milk
     Coarse salt (optional)
  1 large English cucumber, very thinly sliced
 10 radishes, very thinly sliced
     Small fresh thyme sprigs (optional)

1. In a medium bowl combine cheese, green onion, and horseradish; cover and chill until ready to use.

2. Preheat oven to 375°F. Unfold one of the puff pastry sheets on a lightly floured surface. With the tines of a fork, generously prick the pastry. Use a 2-inch triangle, square, or round cutter to cut pastry into 16 shapes. (Do not reroll pastry scraps.) Repeat with remaining puff pastry sheet.

3. Transfer pastries to an ungreased baking sheet. Lightly brush each pastry with milk. If desired, sprinkle with salt. Bake for 10 to 12 minutes or until golden. Cool on a wire rack.

4. To assemble, use a knife to split the baked pastries horizontally. Spread about 1 teaspoon of the cheese mixture onto the cut side of each bottom pastry. Top with a cucumber slice and some radish slices. Spread about 1 teaspoon of the cheese mixture onto the cut side of each pastry top. Place on top of radish slices. If desired, garnish each sandwich with a thyme sprig.

Per sandwich: 112 cal., 8 g total fat (3 g sat. fat), 4 mg chol., 75 mg sodium, 8 g carbo., 0 g fiber, 3 g pro.

Cucumber Canapés

Lemon, in the form of shredded peel and juice, adds a subtle flavor to these cucumber sandwiches. See photo, page 123.

Start to Finish: 30 minutes **Makes:** 24 appetizers

  ½ of a medium English cucumber,
     very thinly sliced (1 cup)
  ½ cup thinly sliced red onion
  ½ teaspoon finely shredded lemon peel
  2 teaspoons lemon juice
  ¼ teaspoon salt
  6 slices firm-textured white and/or
     whole wheat bread
  ¼ cup butter or margarine, softened
  ½ cup dairy sour cream
  1 tablespoon snipped fresh chives

1. In a bowl combine cucumber, red onion, lemon peel, lemon juice, salt, and ¼ teaspoon *ground black pepper*; toss gently to combine.

2. If desired, remove crusts from bread slices. Cut each bread slice diagonally into quarters. (Or use 2- to 2½-inch decorative cutters to cut shapes from bread slices.) Spread butter onto one side of each piece of bread; top each with some of the cucumber mixture.

3. In a small bowl combine sour cream and chives. Spoon a little of the sour cream mixture on top of each canape. If desired, garnish each canape with additional *finely shredded lemon peel*. Serve immediately or cover and chill for up to 2 hours.

Per appetizer: 45 cal., 3 g total fat (2 g sat. fat), 7 mg chol., 74 mg sodium, 4 g carbo., 0 g fiber, 1 g pro.

Garden-Style
Puff Pastry
Sandwiches

new year's eve favorites

No matter how you celebrate New Year's Eve, here are recipes to make it festive. Whether you host a formal cocktail party, a sit-down dinner, or a casual all-ages gathering, you will find great options in this chapter: mouthwatering appetizers, beverages, and a champagne cake too.

New Year's Champagne Cake,
page 140

Shrimp and Avocado Cocktail

Orange sections and avocado pieces plus horseradish, peppers, and fresh cilantro introduce a lively diversion from the traditional, tomato-based cocktail.

Prep: 30 minutes **Chill:** 2 hours
Makes: 8 to 10 appetizer servings

1½	pounds fresh or frozen large shrimp in shells
¼	cup ketchup
2	tablespoons orange juice
1	tablespoon salad oil
2	teaspoons prepared horseradish
⅛	teaspoon salt
⅛	teaspoon cayenne pepper
2	avocados, halved, seeded, peeled, and finely chopped
1	medium orange, peeled and sectioned or ½ of an 11-ounce can mandarin orange sections, drained
1	tablespoon snipped fresh cilantro
1	fresh jalapeño chile pepper, seeded and finely chopped (see Note, page 58)
	Torn mixed salad greens

1. Thaw shrimp, if frozen. Peel and devein shrimp. Cook shrimp in lightly salted boiling water for 1 to 3 minutes or until shrimp turn opaque, stirring occasionally. Drain; rinse under cold running water. Drain well. Cover and chill shrimp for at least 2 hours or overnight.

2. For dressing, in a screw-top jar combine ketchup, orange juice, salad oil, horseradish, salt, and cayenne pepper. Cover and shake well. Pour dressing over shrimp, tossing to coat. In a medium bowl combine avocados, orange sections, cilantro, and jalapeño pepper.

3. To serve, line 8 to 10 chilled martini glasses or individual salad plates with salad greens. Top with avocado mixture and shrimp. Serve immediately.

Per serving: 188 cal., 10 g total fat (2 g sat. fat), 86 mg chol., 213 mg sodium, 12 g carbo., 5 g fiber, 14 g pro.

Savory Shrimp Pâté

This savory meat spread is made with shrimp rather than chicken liver. Pâté lovers and those who don't care for stronger-flavored liver may come to prefer it.

Prep: 20 minutes **Chill:** 2 hours
Makes: 36 appetizers

⅓	cup plain yogurt
1	3-ounce package cream cheese, cut into cubes
⅓	cup chopped green onions
1	tablespoon horseradish mustard
1½	teaspoons finely shredded lemon peel
1	teaspoon dried dill
½	teaspoon sugar
½	teaspoon bottled hot pepper sauce
¼	teaspoon salt
12	ounces cooked shrimp
36	crackers and/or 2-inch pieces of celery

1. In a food processor combine yogurt and cream cheese. Cover and process until combined. Add green onions, horseradish mustard, lemon peel, dill, sugar, hot pepper sauce, and salt. Cover and process until nearly smooth. Add shrimp. Cover and process with on/off pulses until shrimp is finely chopped. Transfer pâté to a medium bowl. Cover and chill for 2 to 24 hours.

2. To serve, pipe or spread pâté onto crackers and/or celery pieces.

Per appetizer (pâté only): 34 cal., 2 g total fat (1 g sat. fat), 21 mg chol., 74 mg sodium, 2 g carbo., 0 g fiber, 3 g pro.

Shrimp and Avocado Cocktail

Southern Pimiento Cheese and Pork Spread

Remember pimiento cheese spread? Revive your affection for it by mixing in smoked cheese, ground pork, and of course, pimiento.

Prep: 20 minutes **Chill:** 2 hours
Makes: about 3½ cups spread

4	ounces ground pork
⅛	teaspoon cayenne pepper
2	cups shredded smoked cheddar cheese
1¼	cups finely shredded Parmesan cheese
½	cup chopped pimiento or roasted red sweet peppers
2	tablespoons finely chopped green onion
1	cup mayonnaise or salad dressing
1	tablespoon cider vinegar
¼	teaspoon ground black pepper
⅛	teaspoon salt
	Assorted crackers

1. In a small skillet cook pork over medium heat until brown; drain well. Transfer pork to a large bowl; stir in cayenne pepper. Cool slightly. Stir cheddar cheese, Parmesan cheese, pimiento, and green onion into cooled pork. In a small bowl combine mayonnaise, vinegar, black pepper, and salt; stir into pork mixture. Cover and chill for 2 to 24 hours. Serve with crackers.

Per 2 tablespoons: 116 cal., 11 g total fat (4 g sat. fat), 17 mg chol., 168 mg sodium, 1 g carbo., 0 g fiber, 4 g pro.

Southern Pimiento Cheese and Pork Spread

Cheese Truffles

Move over chocolate. In this recipe, rich cheese is rolled in a ball and coated with finely snipped herbs, nuts, peppercorns, or bread crumbs.

Prep: 45 minutes **Chill:** 5 hours **Makes:** 30 truffles

1	8-ounce package cream cheese, softened
½	cup finely shredded Monterey Jack cheese or Muenster cheese
⅛	teaspoon cayenne pepper
2	to 3 ounces Gorgonzola cheese or smoked Gouda cheese

Desired coatings (such as finely chopped pistachio nuts, finely snipped fresh herbs, finely crushed tricolor peppercorns, and/or toasted pumpernickel bread crumbs)

1. In a medium bowl stir together cream cheese, Monterey Jack cheese, and cayenne pepper. Cover and chill about 1 hour or until easy to handle.

2. Cut Gorgonzola cheese into 30 small pieces. Working with a scant 2 teaspoons of the cream cheese mixture at a time, form a small ball of cream cheese mixture around a piece of the Gorgonzola cheese. (If cream cheese mixture becomes too soft, chill until easy to handle.) Roll in desired coatings. Cover and chill for up to 4 hours.

Per truffle: 40 cal., 4 g total fat (2 g sat. fat), 11 mg chol., 59 mg sodium, 0 g carbo., 0 g fiber, 1 g pro.

Italian-Style
Relish Tray

Italian-Style Relish Tray

This is a sophisticated tray of bite-size appetizer roll varieties paired with roasted sweet peppers, artichoke hearts, olives, capers, and bread.

Start to Finish: 30 minutes
Makes: 12 appetizer servings

1   **recipe Salami Rolls**
1   **recipe Italian Cheese Bites**
1   **7-ounce jar roasted red and/or yellow**
    sweet peppers, drained and cut into strips
2   **6-ounce jars marinated artichoke hearts,**
    drained
8   **ounces pitted green or ripe olives, drained**
    Capers
    Thinly sliced ciabatta or Italian bread
    (optional)

1. Arrange Salami Rolls, Italian Cheese Bites, sweet pepper strips, artichoke hearts, and olives on a serving platter. Sprinkle capers over artichoke hearts. If desired, serve with ciabatta.

Salami Rolls: Spread each of 24 thin slices garlic salami (about 4 ounces) with ½ teaspoon kalamata olive tapenade (¼ cup total). Place a roasted red sweet pepper strip along one edge of each salami slice; roll up. Cut in half crosswise.

Italian Cheese Bites: Cut 4 ounces thinly sliced prosciutto into narrow strips. Cut 1½ pounds taleggio, Asiago, and/or aged provolone cheese into bite-size pieces. Wrap a prosciutto strip around each piece of cheese.

Per serving: 426 cal., 37 g total fat (17 g sat. fat), 69 mg chol., 1,406 mg sodium, 6 g carbo., 1 g fiber, 19 g pro.

Pomegranate Champagne Cocktail

Pomegranate juice is taking over the juice aisle. Let it join your party in a festive flute too.

Start to Finish: 5 minutes **Makes:** 3 servings

> 3 ounces chilled pomegranate juice or cranberry juice
> 9 ounces chilled Champagne

1. Divide pomegranate juice among 3 champagne flutes; slowly add 3 ounces Champagne to each flute. Serve immediately.

Per serving: 76 cal., 0 g total fat (0 g sat. fat), 0 mg chol., 2 mg sodium, 6 g carbo., 0 g fiber, 0 g pro.

Cranberry Martinis

Make your own cranberry-flavor vodka to serve as a fine finish to the year. The vodka can be made up to 3 days ahead.

Prep: 20 minutes **Cool:** 30 minutes **Freeze:** 3 days
Makes: 8 servings

> 1 cup cranberries
> 1 cup sugar
> 1 cup water
> 1 750-milliliter bottle good-quality vodka
> Sugar
> Ice cubes
> Cranberries (optional)

1. For cranberry-flavor vodka, in a 1½-quart saucepan combine the 1 cup cranberries, the 1 cup sugar, and water. Bring to boiling, stirring until sugar dissolves. Continue cooking just until cranberries start to pop. Remove saucepan from heat; cool 30 minutes. Strain cranberry mixture, reserving cranberries and liquid. In a large glass pitcher combine vodka, strained cranberries, and ⅔ cup of the reserved liquid (discard remaining liquid). Cover and freeze for up to 3 days. Strain cranberries from of vodka; discard cranberries (you should have about 4 cups cranberry vodka).

2. Dip rims of eight martini glasses in water. Dip rims into a dish of sugar to coat; set aside.

3. Place ice cubes in a martini shaker. For four drinks, add 2 cups cranberry vodka; shake. Strain into four of the prepared glasses; repeat. If desired, garnish each glass with additional cranberries threaded onto small skewers.

Per serving: 320 cal., 0 g total fat (0 g sat. fat), 0 mg chol., 2 mg sodium, 30 g carbo., 0 g fiber, 0 g pro.

Champagne Citrus Punch

Orange juice and lemonade concentrates blend with a sweet white wine to give this champagne punch a tart edge.

Start to Finish: 10 minutes
Makes: ten (6-ounce) servings

> 1 6-ounce can (⅔ cup) frozen orange juice concentrate, thawed
> ½ of a 6-ounce can (⅓ cup) frozen lemonade concentrate, thawed
> ½ of a 750-milliliter bottle (about 1⅔ cups) sweet white wine (such as Riesling or white Zinfandel), chilled
> 1 cup cold water
> 1 750-milliliter bottle Champagne, chilled

1. In a punch bowl combine orange juice concentrate and lemonade concentrate. Add wine and water, stirring to combine. Carefully add Champagne but do not stir. Serve immediately.

Per serving: 126 cal., 0 g total fat (0 g sat. fat), 0 mg chol., 2 mg sodium, 14 g carbo., 0 g fiber, 1 g pro.

Cranberry Martinis

Ham Soup with Black-Eyed Peas and Hominy

In the South, ham hock and peas are often on the New Year's Day menu. They are thought to bring good luck.

Prep: 20 minutes **Cook:** 40 minutes
Makes: 4 servings

1	cup chopped celery
1	cup chopped onion
¾	cup chopped green sweet pepper
2	cloves garlic, minced
2	tablespoons olive oil
1¼	cups finely chopped cooked ham
1	teaspoon paprika
½	teaspoon sugar
½	teaspoon dry mustard
½	teaspoon ground cumin
½	teaspoon dried basil, crushed
½	teaspoon dried oregano, crushed
½	teaspoon dried thyme, crushed
¼	teaspoon ground cloves
¼	teaspoon ground black pepper
⅛	teaspoon cayenne pepper
1	15½-ounce can black-eyed peas, rinsed and drained
1	14½-ounce can golden hominy, rinsed and drained
1	14½-ounce can diced tomatoes, undrained
1	14-ounce can chicken broth
1	tablespoon snipped fresh parsley
1	tablespoon mild-flavor molasses

1. In a 4-quart Dutch oven cook and stir celery, onion, sweet pepper, and garlic in hot oil over medium heat for 5 minutes. Stir in ham, paprika, sugar, dry mustard, cumin, basil, oregano, thyme, cloves, black pepper, and cayenne pepper. Cook and stir for 5 minutes more.

2. Stir black-eyed peas, hominy, undrained tomatoes, broth, parsley, and molasses into Dutch oven. Bring to boiling; reduce heat. Simmer, covered, for 30 minutes.

Per serving: 384 cal., 14 g total fat (3 g sat. fat), 24 mg chol., 1,627 mg sodium, 47 g carbo., 10 g fiber, 17 g pro.

Creamy Ham and New Potato Soup

Quartered new potatoes give this creamy vegetable soup a chunky quality too. Cubes of ham make a pretty pink addition that lends a salty tang and makes it a one-bowl party meal.

Start to Finish: 30 minutes **Makes:** 4 servings

12	ounces tiny new potatoes, quartered (2 cups)
1	cup water
1	cup chopped carrot
½	cup chopped onion
½	cup chopped celery
¼	teaspoon dried thyme or basil, crushed, or dried dill
¼	teaspoon white or ground black pepper
1½	cups half-and-half, light cream, or milk
1	10¾-ounce can reduced-fat and reduced-sodium condensed cream of celery or cream of mushroom soup
1	cup cubed cooked ham
¾	cup shredded American cheese

1. In a large saucepan combine potatoes, water, carrot, onion, celery, thyme, and pepper. Bring to boiling; reduce heat. Simmer, covered, for 10 to 15 minutes or until potatoes are tender.

2. Stir half-and-half, soup, and ham into saucepan; heat through. Do not boil. Reduce heat to low; add cheese, stirring until melted.

Per serving: 382 cal., 21 g total fat (12 g sat. fat), 76 mg chol., 1,098 mg sodium, 32 g carbo., 4 g fiber, 16 g pro.

Spicy Beef Short Ribs

Give short ribs a boil, then a lengthy simmer in beer and they will emerge moist and full of flavor. Serve with mashed potatoes or quick-to-fix creamy polenta.

Prep: 10 minutes **Cook:** 1½ hours
Broil: 15 minutes **Makes:** 6 servings

4	to 5 pounds beef short ribs, cut into serving-size pieces
2	12-ounce cans beer
1	cup ketchup

Ham Soup with Black-Eyed Peas
and Hominy

⅓ cup lemon juice
¼ cup packed brown sugar
¼ cup vinegar
3 tablespoons butter or margarine
1 tablespoon Worcestershire sauce
1 tablespoon yellow mustard
1 teaspoon onion powder
½ teaspoon celery seeds
½ teaspoon bottled hot pepper sauce

1. Trim fat from ribs. Place ribs in a 6-quart Dutch oven. Pour beer over ribs. Bring to boiling; reduce heat to low. Simmer, covered, about 1½ hours or until ribs are tender.

2. Meanwhile, for sauce, in a medium saucepan stir together ketchup, lemon juice, brown sugar, vinegar, butter, Worcestershire sauce, mustard, onion powder, celery seeds, and hot pepper sauce. Bring to boiling; reduce heat. Simmer, uncovered, over medium heat for 10 to 15 minutes or until desired consistency, stirring often.

3. Preheat broiler. Place ribs on the greased unheated rack of a broiler pan. Brush ribs with some of the sauce. Broil 4 to 5 inches from heat for 8 minutes. Turn ribs over; brush with more sauce. Broil about 7 minutes more or until heated through. Heat remaining sauce and serve with ribs.

Per serving: 295 cal., 16 g total fat (6 g sat. fat), 73 mg chol., 725 mg sodium, 11 g carbo., 1 g fiber, 26 g pro.

Individual
Pork Wellingtons

Individual Pork Wellingtons

Prep: 30 minutes **Bake:** 25 minutes
Stand: 5 minutes **Oven:** 425°F **Makes:** 4 servings

- 1 **pound pork tenderloin**
- 1 **tablespoon cooking oil**
- ½ **of a 17.3-ounce package frozen puff pastry (1 sheet), thawed**
- 8 **thin slices prosciutto**
- ¼ **cup semisoft cheese with garlic and herb**
- 1 **egg, lightly beaten**
- 1 **tablespoon water**

1. Slice the tenderloin crosswise into 4 pieces. In a medium skillet cook tenderloin pieces in hot oil over medium-high heat until brown, turning once. Drain on paper towels; set aside.

2. Preheat oven to 425°F. Unfold puff pastry; place on a lightly floured surface. Roll into an 11-inch square; cut into four 5½-inch squares. Place one slice of prosciutto in center of each square; top with a pork piece. Top each pork piece with 1 tablespoon of the cheese and another slice of prosciutto. Brush pastry edges with water. Gather corners of pastry over meat. Pinch edges to seal. Combine egg and water; brush over bundles.

3. Place bundles, seam sides up, on a greased baking sheet. Bake, uncovered, about 25 minutes or until pastry is golden brown and thermometer inserted near the center of the pork registers 155°F. Let stand 5 minutes before serving.

Per serving: 672 cal., 44 g total fat (10 g sat. fat), 139 mg chol., 858 mg sodium, 28 g carbo., 1 g fiber, 40 g pro.

Kielbasa and Kraut Skillet

Start to Finish: 25 minutes **Makes:** 4 servings

- 1 **pound cooked kielbasa, bias-sliced into 2-inch pieces**
- 1 **small red onion, thinly sliced**
- 1 **15-ounce can sauerkraut**
- 1 **tablespoon coarse-grain brown mustard**
- ¼ **to ½ teaspoon caraway seeds**
- ¼ **teaspoon salt**
- ¼ **teaspoon ground black pepper**

1. In a large skillet cook kielbasa and onion until onion is just tender. Stir in undrained sauerkraut, mustard, caraway seeds, salt, and pepper. Cook, covered, over medium heat about 10 minutes or until heated through.

Per serving: 392 cal., 34 g total fat (16 g sat. fat), 50 mg chol., 1,755 mg sodium, 6 g carbo., 2 g fiber, 14 g pro.

Black Bean Lasagna

Skip the meat this New Year's with a south-of-the-border-style vegetarian casserole loaded with plenty of flavor.

Prep: 45 minutes **Bake:** 35 minutes
Stand: 10 minutes **Oven:** 350°F **Makes:** 8 servings

 9 **dried lasagna noodles**
 2 **15-ounce cans black beans,**
    rinsed and drained
 1 **egg, lightly beaten**
 1 **12-ounce container cottage cheese**
 1 **8-ounce package cream cheese, cut into**
    cubes and softened
1½ **cups shredded Monterey Jack cheese**
 1 **cup chopped onion**
 ¾ **cup chopped green sweet pepper**
 2 **cloves garlic, minced**
 1 **tablespoon cooking oil**
 1 **15-ounce can Italian-style tomato sauce**
 4 **teaspoons dried cilantro, crushed**
 1 **teaspoon ground cumin**
    Coarsely chopped tomatoes

1. Cook lasagna noodles according to package directions; drain. Rinse noodles with cold water; drain well. Set aside. In a small bowl mash one can of the beans with a potato masher; set aside. In a medium bowl combine egg, cottage cheese, cream cheese, and 1 cup of the Monterey Jack cheese; set aside.

2. In a large skillet cook onion, sweet pepper, and garlic in hot oil over medium-high heat until tender. Stir in mashed beans, the remaining can of whole beans, tomato sauce, cilantro, and cumin; heat through.

3. Preheat oven to 350°F. Arrange 3 of the noodles in a lightly greased 3-quart rectangular baking dish. Top with one-third (about 1⅓ cups) of the bean mixture. Spoon half (about 1 cup) of the cheese mixture over bean mixture. Repeat layers. Top with remaining noodles and bean mixture.

4. Bake, covered, for 35 to 40 minutes or until heated through. Sprinkle with the remaining ½ cup Monterey Jack cheese. Let stand for 10 minutes before serving. Sprinkle with chopped tomatoes.

Per serving: 454 cal., 22 g total fat (12 g sat. fat), 83 mg chol., 857 mg sodium, 45 g carbo., 8 g fiber, 25 g pro.

Black Bean
Lasagna

New Year's Champagne Cake

Go ahead, make this classic cake by starting with a cake mix. Then if you like, make it special by tinting the batter for one of the cake layers with red food coloring.

Prep: 20 minutes **Bake:** 30 minutes
Cool: 10 minutes **Oven:** 350°F **Makes:** 10 servings

1   **2-layer-size white cake mix**
    Champagne or sparkling wine
    Few drops red food coloring
2   **16-ounce cans vanilla frosting**
    Fresh strawberries

1. Preheat oven to 350°F. Grease and lightly flour two 8×1½-inch round cake pans; set aside.

2. Prepare cake mix according to package directions, except replace water with Champagne. Spread batter into prepared pans. Bake for 30 to 35 minutes or until a wooden toothpick inserted in center comes out clean. Cool in pans on wire racks for 10 minutes. Remove cake layers from pans. Cool thoroughly on wire racks.

3. Stir a few drops of food coloring into frosting to make a light pink color. Frost tops and sides with frosting. Garnish with strawberries.

Per serving: 660 cal., 25 g total fat (5 g sat. fat), 0 mg chol., 507 mg sodium, 104 g carbo., 1 g fiber, 3 g pro.

New Year's
Champagne Cake

Pumpkin Spice
Crème Brûlée

Pumpkin Spice Crème Brûlée

You know rich crème brûlée with its hard sugar top and creamy melt-on-your-tongue custard. Try it with pumpkin and pie spices for a just-as-luscious holiday variation.

Prep: 20 minutes **Bake:** 30 minutes
Stand: 20 minutes **Chill:** 1 hour **Makes:** 6 servings

2	cups whipping cream
3	egg yolks, lightly beaten
2	eggs, lightly beaten
⅓	cup sugar
½	cup canned pumpkin
1	teaspoon ground cinnamon
1	teaspoon ground ginger
¼	teaspoon ground cloves
¼	cup sugar

1. Preheat oven to 350°F. In a small heavy saucepan heat whipping cream over medium-low heat just until bubbly. Remove from heat; set aside.

2. Meanwhile, in a medium bowl combine egg yolks, eggs, the ⅓ cup sugar, pumpkin, cinnamon, ginger, and cloves. Beat with a wire whisk or rotary beater just until combined. Slowly whisk the hot whipping cream into the egg mixture.

3. Place six ¾-cup soufflé dishes or 6-ounce custard cups in a 3-quart rectangular baking pan. Divide custard mixture evenly among the soufflé dishes. Place baking pan on oven rack. Pour enough boiling water into the baking pan to reach halfway up the sides of the soufflé dishes.

4. Bake about 30 minutes or until a knife inserted near centers comes out clean. Carefully remove pan from oven. Remove dishes from water; cool on a wire rack. Cover and chill for at least 1 hour or up to 8 hours.

5. Before serving, let custards stand at room temperature for 20 minutes. Meanwhile, in an 8-inch heavy skillet heat the ¼ cup sugar over medium-high heat until sugar begins to melt, shaking skillet occasionally to heat sugar evenly. Do not stir. Once sugar starts to melt, reduce heat to low and cook for 3 to 5 minutes more or until all of the sugar is melted and golden, stirring as needed with a wooden spoon.

6. Quickly drizzle caramelized sugar over the custards. (If sugar hardens in skillet, return to heat; stir until melted.) Serve immediately.

Per serving: 412 cal., 34 g total fat (20 g sat. fat), 287 mg chol., 57 mg sodium, 23 g carbo., 1 g fiber, 5 g pro.

chocolate
town

Chocolate houses are among
the easiest to make—simply
build each house out of candy
bars, using melted chocolate
for glue. Add your favorite
embellishments, then create
a snowy scene and arrange the
houses to form a tiny village.

Chocolate Town,
pages 144-147

Chocolate House

Start to Finish: 1 hour **Makes:** 1 house

4   8- or 5-ounce milk chocolate bars
      Chocolate creme-filled pirouette cookies
2   to 3 100-calorie packs baked chocolate
      wafer snacks
      Chocolate-covered espresso beans
      Miniature layered chocolate-mint candies
1   2-ounce package (2 bars) chocolate-
      covered caramel-topped cookie bars
      Pretzel sticks
      Chocolate coin
      Semisweet chocolate pieces
      Coarse sugar
      Chocolate Snowman (page 145) (optional)
      Chocolate Pine Trees (page 145) (optional)

1. Unwrap chocolate bars; set on a cutting board.
Use a small serrated knife to carefully cut two
of the chocolate bars with the "Front and Back"
pattern (see patterns, pages 146–147) (cut slowly

Chocolate House

and gently so the chocolate doesn't crack or break).
Set aside scrap pieces of chocolate. Cut a third
chocolate bar in half crosswise for the "Side"
patterns. Cut the remaining chocolate bar in half
for the "Roof" patterns. Line a baking sheet with
foil or waxed paper; set aside.

2. Break scrap chocolate pieces into smaller bits;
place in a microwave-safe bowl. Microwave on
50 percent power (medium) for 1 to 2 minutes
or until melted, stirring every 30 seconds. Place
slightly cooled melted chocolate in a resealable
plastic bag; seal bag. Cut a small hole in one
corner of the bag.

3. On prepared baking sheet, use tumblers to hold
chocolate pieces in place while assembling. Attach
the inside edge of a Side wall to the outside edge
of a Front wall by piping some of the melted
chocolate between the two edges that meet; press
pieces firmly together. Attach the other inside edge
of a Side wall to the outside edge of a Front wall
by piping melted chocolate where the two edges
meet; press firmly. Finally, attach the outside edges
of the Back piece to the inside edges of the two
Side pieces by piping melted chocolate where the
two edges meet; press firmly. Hold pieces together
with tumblers until chocolate is set.

4. Attach the roof pieces with melted chocolate
(if chocolate cools and hardens, microwave on
50 percent power [medium] about 30 seconds or
until smooth). If pieces won't fit together perfectly;
fill in any holes and gaps with melted chocolate.
Hold roof pieces in place with tumblers until
chocolate is set. Pipe more melted chocolate along
seams where roof pieces attach to front and back
pieces; attach pirouette cookies.

5. To add shingles to the roof, pipe melted
chocolate along the bottom of a roof piece. Add a
row of chocolate wafer snacks. Pipe more melted
chocolate above and on the very top portion of
the row of wafers; attach another row of wafers,
overlapping the next row over the previous row.
Pipe more melted chocolate and rows of wafers
until roof piece is covered; repeat steps with the
other roof piece.

6. To decorate, pipe melted chocolate along the
bottom outside edge of house; attach chocolate-
covered espresso beans in a row along base of

Chocolate Candy House

Chocolate Nut House

house. For windows, use melted chocolate to attach miniature layered chocolate-mint candies to the front and sides of house. For the door, cut one chocolate-covered caramel-topped cookie bar in half crosswise; attach with melted chocolate. Frame with pretzel sticks; attach chocolate coin above door. Cover corner seams with chocolate pieces.

7. Set Chocolate House on a clean cutting board, baking sheet, or other desired flat display surface. For snow, sprinkle coarse sugar around the base of the house. If desired, decorate with a Chocolate Snowman and Chocolate Pine Trees.

Chocolate Candy House: Create Chocolate House as directed, except use melted chocolate to attach different candies for decoration. For example, use 2 sticks of chewing gum for door. Frame with small red, green, and white candies; attach a starlight mint above door. Use a peppermint stick for top of roof; peppermint pillows along roof for trim; and pastel wafer candies (such as Necco wafers) for shingles. Break the "hook" off candy canes and use for the windows on sides and back of house; use the straight part to cover corner seams.

Chocolate Nut House: Create Chocolate House as directed, except use melted chocolate to attach different nuts for decoration. For example, use a graham cracker for door with an end piece of a sliced almond as a doorknob. Attach slivered almonds and pepitas around base of house and use sliced almonds as shingles, with pepitas for color accents. Use a chocolate-covered pretzel rod for a chimney; whole almonds for windows on side of

house, accented with small red candies. Use 2 pecan halves for windows on front of house, accented with pine nuts. Use cashews as decoration above door and peanuts along roof for trim.

Chocolate Snowman: Place a wire rack over waxed paper. Dip 2 large marshmallows in melted vanilla-flavor candy coating. Let stand on rack until set. Attach the 2 marshmallows with a toothpick for the snowman body. Add pretzel sticks for arms. If desired, use melted candy coating to attach 1 white chocolate kiss with stripes for a hat and miniature chocolate chips for eyes, mouth, and buttons.

Chocolate Pine Trees: Place a wire rack over waxed paper. Dip desired number of rolled sugar ice-cream cones in melted chocolate, coating completely. If desired, sprinkle with white edible glitter, chocolate sprinkles, or nonpareils. Let stand on rack until set.

CHOCOLATE HOUSE
ROOF AND SIDES
(make four)

Patterns for 8-ounce
milk chocolate bars

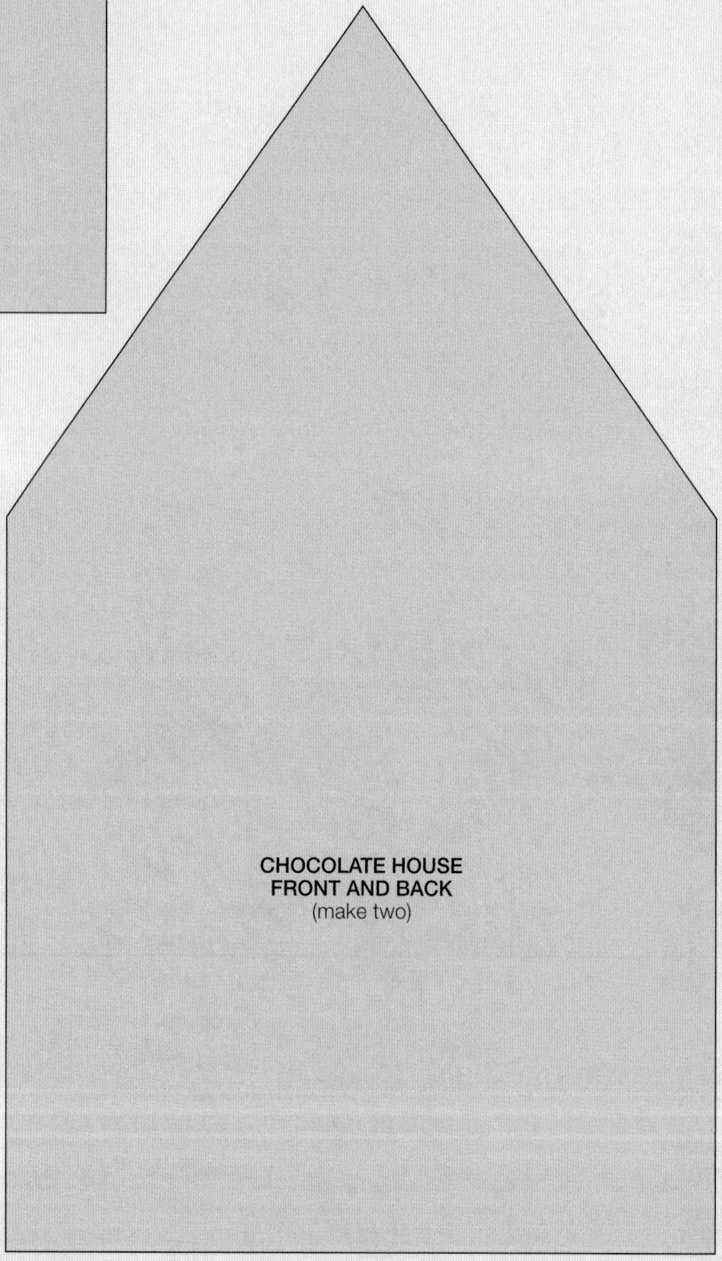

CHOCOLATE HOUSE
FRONT AND BACK
(make two)

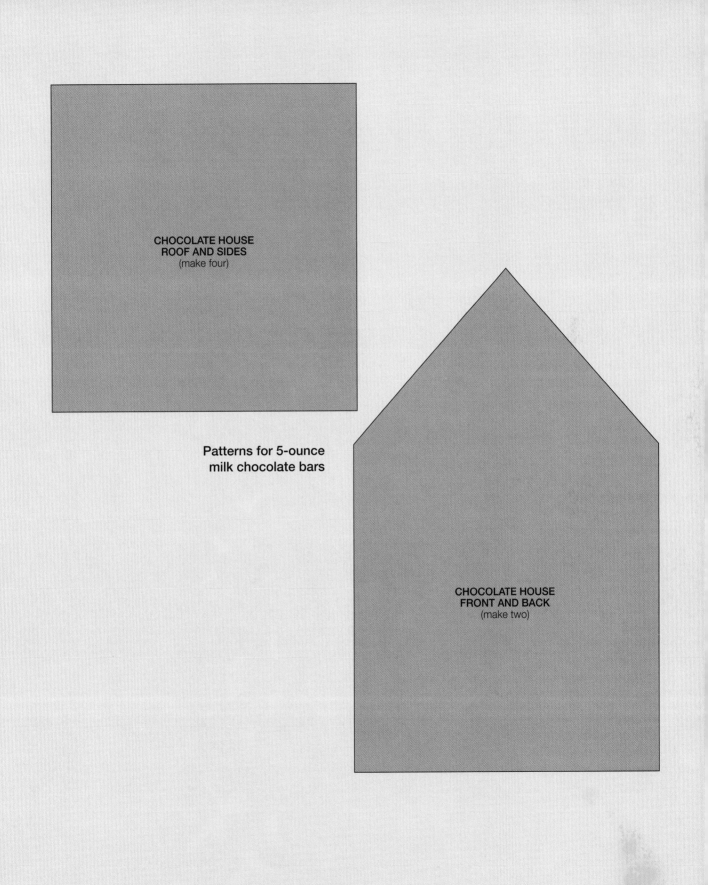

CHOCOLATE HOUSE
ROOF AND SIDES
(make four)

Patterns for 5-ounce
milk chocolate bars

CHOCOLATE HOUSE
FRONT AND BACK
(make two)

candy cane pizzazz

Jazz up classic cutout cookies with red and white frostings, peppermint pillows, and sparkling sugars. Arrange the cookies on a platter for a merry and bright presentation.

Candy Cane
Sugar Cookies,
page 150

Candy Cane Sugar Cookies

Prep: 30 minutes **Bake:** 7 minutes per batch
Chill: 30 minutes **Oven:** 375°F
Makes: seventy-two to eighty-four 2-inch cookies
or forty-eight 4-inch cookies

⅔   cup butter, softened
¾   cup sugar
1   teaspoon baking powder
¼   teaspoon salt
1   egg
1   tablespoon milk
1   teaspoon vanilla
2   cups all-purpose flour
1   recipe Powdered Sugar Icing and/or
    Creamy White Frosting (page 151)

1. Preheat oven to 375°F. In a large mixing bowl beat butter on medium to high speed 30 seconds. Add sugar, baking powder, and salt. Beat until combined, scraping bowl. Beat in egg, milk, and vanilla until combined. Beat in as much of the flour as you can. Stir in any remaining flour. Divide dough in half. If necessary, cover and chill dough about 30 minutes or until easy to handle.

2. On a lightly floured surface, roll half the dough at a time to ⅛ inch thick. Use a 2- or 4-inch candy-cane-shape cookie cutter to cut dough. Place cutouts 1 inch apart on an ungreased cookie sheet.

3. Bake for 7 to 8 minutes or until edges are firm and bottoms are very light brown. Transfer to a wire rack and let cool. If desired, tint some of the Powdered Sugar Icing and/or Creamy White Frosting with *red paste food coloring*. Decorate as desired with *decorating gel, peppermint pillows,* and/or *sanding sugar.*

Per 2-inch cookie: 40 cal., 2 g total fat (1 g sat. fat), 7 mg chol., 25 mg sodium, 6 g carbo., 0 g fiber, 0 g pro.

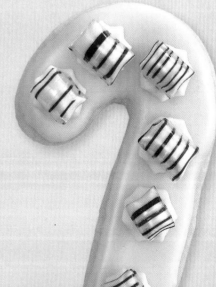

Creamy White Frosting

For a bright white frosting, use clear vanilla.

Start to Finish: 25 minutes **Makes:** about 3 cups

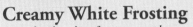

1	**cup shortening**
1½	**teaspoons vanilla**
½	**teaspoon almond extract**
1	**pound powdered sugar (about 4 cups)**
3	**to 4 tablespoons milk**

1. In a large mixing bowl beat shortening, vanilla, and almond extract with an electric mixer on medium speed for 30 seconds. Slowly add about half of the powdered sugar, beating well. Add 2 tablespoons of the milk. Gradually beat in remaining powdered sugar and enough remaining milk to reach spreading consistency.

Per 24 (2 tablespoon) servings: 149 cal., 8 g total fat (g sat. fat), 0 mg chol., 1 mg sodium, 19 g carbo., 0 g fiber, 0 g pro.

Powdered Sugar Icing

Start to Finish: 10 minutes
Makes: about 1 cup

2	**cups powdered sugar**
½	**teaspoon vanilla**
2	**tablespoons milk**

1. In a small bowl combine powdered sugar, vanilla, and milk. Stir in additional milk, 1 teaspoon at a time, until icing reaches desired consistency.

Per 12 (2 teaspoon) servings: 80 cal., 0 g total fat (0 g sat. fat), 0 mg chol., 1 mg sodium, 20 g carbo., 0 g fiber, 0 g pro.

party planner
menus

Do you want some help putting menus together?
On the following pages you will find several
creative party suggestions along with full menu
ideas to use or inspire your own plans. Pace
yourself though. For most, successful entertaining
is like party dressing: rely on your favorites and
introduce new elements one or two at a time.
The point is to enjoy every moment, so avoid
planning more than you can do easily.

menu 1

Southern Holiday Dinner for 8–10

From ham to sweet potatoes, corn bread stuffing to biscuits, this homecoming holiday menu fills your table and home with texture, flavor, and savory aromas.

Spice-Rubbed Ham with Apple-Maple Sauce, page 10

Glazed Sweet Potatoes, page 33

Steamed broccoli*

Chopped Holiday Salad, page 18

Cranberry-Apple Corn Bread Stuffing, page 24

Buttermilk biscuits*

Chocolate Chess Pie, page 81

Lime-Infused Coconut Pound Cake, page 86

*generic recipes

menu 2

Farm-Style Holiday Feast for 8–10

Savory, soft, crisp, creamy, rich, spicy, and sweet all play together in this symphony of flavors. Recipes are at their very best to satisfy those who sit down to this celebratory meal.

Maple-Brined Turkey, page 13

Green Bean Casserole with Crispy Shallots, page 27

Sour Cream and Chive Mashed Potatoes, page 30

Brown Bread Stuffing, page 23

Mixed greens salad*

Dinner rolls*

Pumpkin-Apple Butter Pie, page 82

Country-Style Pear and Mincemeat Tart, page 82

*generic recipes

menu 3

Fiesta Appetizer Party for 10–12

If your crowd loves chips, salsa, and cheese dip, then treat them to snappy, sophisticated versions of that flavor family. A savory-sweet cookie offers a nifty finish.

Roasted Tomatillo and Jalapeño Guacamole, page 40

Chipotle-Cheddar Cheesecake with Chunky Salsa, page 42

Chipotle Chicken Meatballs, page 48

Cheddar-Jelly Thumbprints, page 47

Roasted pepitas*

Frozen margaritas,* bottled Mexican beer, soft drinks

*generic recipes

menu 4

Holiday Brunch for 6

Who doesn't love brunches on weekends and during vacations? They are a lovely way to slip in camaraderie before enjoying a full day and so conducive to multigenerational groups as well.

Make-Ahead Brunch Lasagna Rolls, page 58

Gingerbread-Sour Cream Muffins, page 74

Mixed fruit compote*

Crisp-cooked bacon*

Pomegranate Spritzers, page 36

Minty Cocoa, page 38

*generic recipes

menu 5

Ringing in the New Year Cocktail Party for 12

*Elegant specialties star in a menu that is simultaneously light, rich,
and full of sophisticated flavors.*

Savory Shrimp Pâté, page 132

Sensational Stuffed Portobellos, page 48

Panzanella Bruschetta, page 46

Herb-Baked Olives**, page 44

Cosmo Fruit Punch, page 36

Champagne

Flavored sparkling water

**double this recipe

menu 6

Dessert Buffet for 16

*Why not host this all-sweets party on a weeknight, inviting guests to stop by
as they come and go from shopping, school concerts, and other holiday activities?*

Gingered Carrot Cake, page 87

Red Velvet Cupcakes with Peppermint Frosting, page 85

Orange-Sugared Snowballs, page 100

Chocolate-Caramel Thumbprints, page 101

Pumpkin-Pecan Cheesecake, page 92

Dark Chocolate Butter Toffee, page 109

Eggnog Punch, page 38

Coffee*

*generic recipes

continued on page 158

continued on page 160